Istanbul Travel Guide 2024

"Discover Istanbul's Iconic Attractions, Vibrant Culture, and Timeless Charm in the Ultimate 2024 Travel Guide!"

Gloria W. Moser

Istanbul Travel Guide 2024

Map of Istanbul

Istanbul Travel Guide 2024

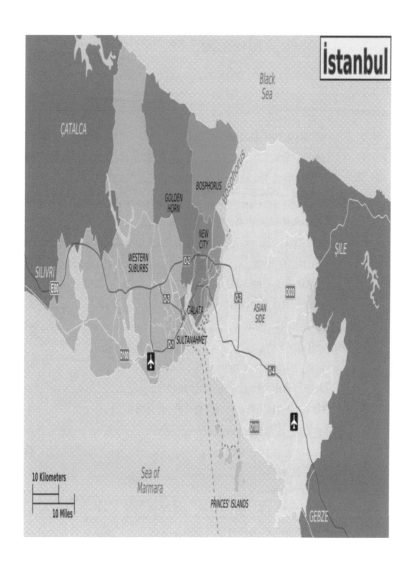

Istanbul Travel Guide 2024

Table of Content

Introduction

As I traveled around Istanbul's historic streets, a

city intertwined with threads of history, culture, and lively energy, I couldn't help but admire the hidden jewels that awaited me at every turn. Allow me to take you on a trip through my eyes, describing the events that transformed Istanbul from a mere map location into a wonderful tapestry of memories.

The voyage started with the excitement of seeing a city where East and West collided, where centuries-old architecture stood proudly alongside new marvels. The enthusiasm was evident when I arrived at Istanbul's Ataturk Airport, a hub for varied cultures and eager passengers. From the airport, the city spread before me like a big novel, with each area representing a chapter with its own distinct appeal.

Wandering around Sultanahmet, I found myself gazing in front of the magnificent Hagia Sophia, a tribute to Istanbul's rich past. The spires and minarets drawn against the sky depicted empires rising and dying, leaving behind a city that saw it all. As the call to prayer resonated through the air, the Blue Mosque appeared, covered with delicate tiles that seemed to convey secrets from ages before.

Navigating the labyrinthine passageways of the Grand Bazaar and Spice Bazaar, I was enveloped in a sensory assault of colors, perfumes, and noises. These vibrant marketplaces provided an insight into Istanbul's essence, where the old and contemporary coexisted together. It was here that I learned the art of negotiating, tasted true Turkish pleasure, and experienced the excitement of discovering hidden riches.

A sail along the Bosphorus becomes a journey through time, with the skyline effortlessly blending palaces, mosques, and contemporary constructions. The sun sinking behind the city silhouette produced a scene that left me in awe, reflecting on the beauty of Istanbul's two continents.

The scent of sizzling kebabs on street corners, along with the sound of traditional Turkish music, prompted me to discover Istanbul's gastronomic treasures. From the spicy joys of Turkish mezes to the sweet extravagance of baklava, each meal was a festival of sensations that danced on my tongue.

As night struck, Istanbul morphed into a distinct entity: a metropolis that never sleeps. The active nightlife, whether in comfortable pubs on Istiklal Avenue or frenetic nightclubs hidden in the backstreets, urged me to join the city's rhythm after dark.

However, Istanbul's fascination was not limited to its monuments and vibrant streets. Day trips to the

---

Istanbul Travel Guide 2024

Princes' Islands and the ancient city of Ephesus showed a side of Istanbul that went beyond the city boundaries, providing a tapestry of experiences that enriched my vacation.

In the heart of this complex and thriving metropolis, I discovered not just a destination but also a riveting narrative begging to be told. Istanbul, with its mix of history, culture, and modernity, is more than simply a destination; it's an immersive experience that begs you to become a part of its story. So, join me as we discover the charm of Istanbul, a city where every moment is a page flipped in the book of a thrilling journey.

Welcome to Istanbul, a city where the past whispers down ancient alleyways and the future plays out in the shadows of minarets. Prepare to be fascinated by a location that seamlessly combines history, culture, and modernity. Istanbul encourages you to be a part of its narrative, with each cobblestone and busy market having its own story to tell. Whether you're attracted to the architectural marvels of Hagia Sophia and the Blue Mosque or the colorful energy of the Grand Bazaar, each encounter in Istanbul promises to be the next chapter of a fascinating trip. So, let the city unfold in front of you and immerse yourself in the charm of Istanbul, where East meets West and every moment seems like a new discovery. Welcome to a city that greets you with open arms and promises to make an unforgettable impression on your heart.

Why visit Istanbul in 2024?

Visiting Istanbul in 2024 provides an unforgettable experience that combines the city's historical beauty with contemporary excitement. Here are strong reasons to visit Istanbul this year:

Cultural Tapestry: Istanbul is a live example of Eastern and Western cultures coming together. In 2024, the city will continue to celebrate its rich heritage with awe-inspiring buildings such as Hagia Sophia, the Blue Mosque, and Topkapi Palace, offering a fascinating trip through centuries of civilization.

Dynamic Modernity: Despite its rich past, Istanbul is a city on the move. In 2024, see old buildings juxtaposed alongside modern constructions. The landscape is continually changing, providing a dynamic urban experience complete with contemporary art galleries, fashionable districts, and a booming culinary scene.

Global Events: Throughout the year, Istanbul hosts a variety of international events, festivals, and cultural activities. In 2024, immerse yourself in Istanbul's vibrant atmosphere by visiting concerts, art exhibits, and festivals that highlight the city's diverse and creative cultural landscape.

Epicurean Delights: Treat your taste buds to the delicious tastes of Turkish cuisine. From the heady spices of the Grand Bazaar to the real kebabs sizzling on street corners, Istanbul's culinary delights are a gourmet journey. 2024 is an excellent time to discover the city's numerous eating choices, which range from historic restaurants to cutting-edge culinary places.

A trip around the Bosphorus Strait is still a must-do in Istanbul. In 2024, take in the spectacular vista of the city's skyline, where Europe meets Asia. The glittering seas and ancient structures along the strait make for an amazing tour that encapsulates Istanbul's geographical and cultural importance.

Local celebrations: Enjoy the warmth of Turkish hospitality during local festivals and celebrations. Istanbul's calendar is jam-packed with events, and 2024 provides the opportunity to join in cultural traditions, bustling street fairs, and cheerful gatherings that highlight the city's vivid personality.

Istanbul is progressively embracing ecological and ethical tourism. In 2024, support eco-friendly activities and participate in events that highlight the preservation of the city's natural and cultural heritage.

Day excursions and exploration: Take advantage of Istanbul's strategic position to plan interesting day excursions to surrounding attractions like the Princes' Islands, Troy, and Ephesus. In 2024, expand your investigation outside the city boundaries to experience the different landscapes and historical attractions that surround Istanbul.

As you plan your trip to Istanbul in 2024, imagine a city that perfectly blends history and modernity, providing a rich tapestry of experiences that will leave you with long-lasting memories and a deep connection to this wonderful place.

Chapter One

Getting There.

Getting to Istanbul is a smooth and fascinating experience, with different transit alternatives to suit a variety of interests. Whether you arrive by air, land, or sea, Istanbul's accessibility assures a seamless entry into Turkey's bustling core. In this part, we will look at the many options accessible to tourists, including information on air travel, ground transportation, and visa requirements. Join us as we explore the paths to Istanbul, preparing for a memorable experience in this enchanting city.

Transportation Options

Istanbul's transit choices are numerous and efficient, making it easy to get around. From the minute you arrive, you'll discover a variety of options to suit every taste and travel style. Let's look at the many modes of transportation available to ensure that you can easily navigate the city.

-Air travel

offers air travel to Istanbul via Istanbul Airport

(IST) and Sabiha Gokcen International Airport (SAW).

Flying to Istanbul introduces you to a place where East meets West, and every trip starts with an element of adventure. Istanbul is served by two main airports, each with its own distinct charm and flawless   connection.

Istanbul Airport (IST): Where Modernity Meets Heritage.

Istanbul Airport, located on the city's European side, is a modern hub capable of handling a large number of international aircraft.

Amenities: Istanbul Airport has cutting-edge facilities, including luxury lounges and duty-free shops, to ensure a pleasant and fashionable arrival.

Sabiha Gokcen International Airport (SAW)—A Gateway to the Asian Side:

Sabiha Gokcen International Airport, located on Istanbul's Asian side, provides a unique alternate entrance option.

Convenience: SAW offers fast services, making it an attractive option for those staying on the Asian side or looking for a less congested arrival experience.

Shuttle buses link both airports to the city center, making for a convenient and cost-effective transportation option.

Metro and Taxi Services: A metro line serves

Istanbul Airport, and taxis are widely accessible at both terminals, providing a quick means to reach your destination.

Travel Tips:

Check Flight Options: Istanbul is a significant international hub that provides direct flights from a variety of places worldwide. Explore your choices to discover the most convenient and affordable flights.

Time Zone Considerations: Istanbul works on Turkey Time (TRT), so keep this in mind when arranging your arrival and departure times.

Begin your Istanbul adventure with the expectation that air travel will be more than simply a mode of transportation but rather a precursor to the magical experiences that await you in this enthralling city. As you land in Istanbul, you enter a world where history and modernity mix, beckoning you to be a part of its everlasting tale.

- <u>land or sea.</u>

1.

Buses and Public Transportation: Istanbul's large bus network offers a cost-effective and local way to see the city. Bus stations are deliberately placed, providing an easy method to visit various districts.

The metro system and trams are efficient forms of transportation that link significant sites and neighborhoods. The Marmaray rail travels under the Bosphorus, connecting the European and Asian sides smoothly.

Istanbul Travel Guide 2024

2. Taxis and Ride-Sharing: Taxis are widely accessible in Istanbul, providing a handy and flexible mode of transportation. Check that the taxi has a functional meter or agree on a fee before beginning the ride.

Uber operates in Istanbul, adding an extra degree of comfort and dependability. Using ride-sharing applications might be a convenient choice, particularly for people unfamiliar with the local currency.

3. Renting an automobile: To explore Istanbul and its surroundings independently, automobile rentals are easily accessible. For a seamless driving experience, get familiar with local traffic and parking restrictions.

4. Sea Transportation: Istanbul's ferry system connects the European and Asian shores. Enjoy breathtaking views of the city skyline and the Bosphorus while taking a leisurely ride.

Private Boat Tours: Take a private boat excursion

across Istanbul's canals. Whether sailing the Bosphorus or exploring secret coves, these cruises provide a distinct viewpoint on the city.

Travel Tips:

Istanbulkart: Consider purchasing an Istanbulkart to ensure easy access to public transit. This contactless smart card is compatible with buses, trams, metros, and ferries, making it a convenient and cost-effective mode of transportation.

Traffic Considerations: Istanbul is a thriving city, and traffic may be congested, particularly during peak hours. Plan your trips appropriately to prevent delays.

Embark on a land-and-sea trip in Istanbul, where each means of transportation becomes a vital part of your journey. Whether you're navigating the city's lively streets or sailing down the Bosphorus, the travel itself becomes an exciting part of your Istanbul experience.

-Your visa requirements

1. Entry Regulations and Visa Types: Depending on your nationality, you could need a visa to enter Turkey. Tourist visas, business visas, and e-Visas are among the several kinds of visas.

E-Visa: Many passengers are qualified to apply for an e-Visa, which is available online before arrival. Check the official e-Visa website for eligibility and application instructions.

2. E-Visa Application Process:

Online Applications: Visit the official e-Visa website and complete the online application form.

Payment: Pay the visa fee securely online using one of the approved payment options.

Confirmation: You will get an email confirming your e-Visa, which you must submit upon arrival in Istanbul.

3. Visa on Arrival: Limited eligibility. Certain nations may be eligible for a visa upon arrival. However, it is best to examine the most recent

rules, since policies might change.

4. Visa Extension Possibilities: In rare situations, you may be able to extend your visa while in Turkey. Check with your local immigration authorities for details on extension processes.

5. Passport Requirements:

Validity: Make sure your passport is valid for at least six months after your scheduled travel date.

Blank pages: Check your passport for blank pages to hold visa stamps.

6. Important Considerations:

Advanced Planning: It is essential that you verify visa requirements well ahead of your trip dates to provide enough time for processing.

Official Sources: For the most current and accurate visa information, consult official government websites or consulates.

7. Visa-Free Agreements for Specific Countries: Some nations' citizens are allowed to enter Turkey without a visa for short periods. Check if your

nationality is covered by any visa-free agreements.
Note: Navigating the visa procedure is vital for a successful arrival in Istanbul. To completely enjoy your time in Istanbul, be educated, prepare ahead of time, and follow visa requirements.

-Istanbul Airport Guide

Welcome to Istanbul, where your adventure starts among the excitement of international travel. Istanbul has two main airports, each with its own unique character and attractions. Whether you arrive on the European side at Istanbul Airport (IST) or on the Asian side at Sabiha Gokcen International Airport (SAW), this guide will help you traverse the airports with ease.

-Istanbul Airport (IST): The Gateway to Modern Luxury.

Istanbul Airport, located on the European side of Istanbul, is a large and sophisticated aviation hub.

Facilities:

Luxury Lounges: Enjoy comfort in one of the airport's premium lounges, which include spa services, fine cuisine, and leisure areas.

Shopping Paradise: Duty-free shopping at Istanbul Airport is a luxurious experience, with a diverse selection of worldwide and local brands.

Connectivity: Stay connected with complimentary Wi-Fi and charging stations located throughout the terminal.

-**Sabiha Gokcen International Airport** (SAW) is located on the Asian side of Istanbul, providing a unique access point to the city.

Convenience: SAW's efficient services make it an ideal alternative for tourists looking for a simplified experience.

Shopping and Dining: Visit a variety of stores and restaurants for a sample of local and foreign food.

Connectivity:

-Transport to the city:

Shuttle Services: Both airports provide shuttle

---

services to the city center, making for a cost-effective and handy transfer alternative.

Metro and Taxis: Istanbul Airport features a metro station, and taxis are available at both terminals for a quick ride to your destination.

Tips for a Smooth Experience:

Arrive at the airport early to provide enough time for check-in, security checks, and any waits.

Check Terminal Information: Istanbul Airport has numerous terminals, so be sure you know which one you'll be departing or arriving at in advance.

Customs & Immigration: Prepare for customs and immigration processes, particularly if you are receiving a visa on arrival.

Airport help: If necessary, Istanbul airports offer help services for guests with limited mobility or specific

Chapter Two

Accommodation

In the heart of Istanbul, a myriad of accommodation options awaits, promising not just a place to rest, but an immersive experience that complements the city's rich tapestry. From the historic charm of Sultanahmet to the vibrant energy of Taksim, discover accommodations that seamlessly blend modern comfort with the captivating spirit of Istanbul. This section will guide you through the best neighborhoods to stay in, recommend hotels that cater to diverse preferences, and explore alternative options such as Airbnb, ensuring your stay in Istanbul is as enchanting as the city itself. Welcome to a world where accommodation is not just a place to sleep but an integral part of your Istanbul adventure.

Best Neighborhoods to Stay

1. Sultanahmet - Historic Elegance: Luxury Hotels

Istanbul Travel Guide 2024

Four Seasons Hotel Istanbul at Sultanahmet

- Location: Sultanahmet Square, Old City
- Overview: This luxury hotel seamlessly integrates modern amenities with historic charm. Housed in a former prison, it offers stunning views of Hagia Sophia and the Blue Mosque. Immerse yourself in opulent Turkish decor, indulge in fine dining at Seasons Restaurant, and enjoy a tranquil courtyard setting. Expect exceptional service and proximity to iconic landmarks.
- Cost: Starting from $500 per night

Ajwa Hotel Sultanahmet

- Location: Ahirkapi Sokak, Sultanahmet
- Overview: Ajwa Hotel is a lavish retreat showcasing Ottoman-inspired design. Each room is adorned with handcrafted details, creating an atmosphere of regal elegance. The rooftop terrace provides panoramic views of Istanbul's skyline. The hotel also

houses an exquisite restaurant, Zeferan, serving a fusion of Ottoman, Turkish, and international cuisines.

- Cost: Starting from $600 per night

2. Taksim - Modern Vibes: Boutique Hotels

Gezi Hotel Bosphorus

- Location: Mete Cad. 34, Taksim
- Overview: Nestled in the heart of Taksim, Gezi Hotel Bosphorus combines modern design with eco-friendly practices. Enjoy contemporary art in every room, unwind at the rooftop bar with Bosphorus views, and experience the vibrant energy of Istiklal Avenue just steps away.
- Cost: Starting from $150 per night

Niles Hotel Istanbul

- Location: Asmalı Mescit, Taksim
- Overview: Niles Hotel offers boutique elegance in a lively neighborhood. The hotel boasts a blend of modern and

Ottoman-inspired design. With its central location, you'll have easy access to Taksim Square, Istiklal Avenue, and cultural attractions.

- Cost: Starting from $120 per night

3. Kadikoy - Local Flair: Budget Accommodations

Hush Hostel Lounge

- Location: Caferaga Mahallesi, Kadikoy
- Overview: For budget-conscious travelers, Hush Hostel Lounge in Kadikoy offers a friendly atmosphere and modern amenities. Explore the vibrant Kadikoy district, known for its markets, street art, and diverse culinary scene. The hostel provides both dormitory and private room options.
- Cost: Starting from $30 per night

Moda Drei Hotel

- Location: Moda, Kadikoy
- Overview: Moda Drei Hotel provides budget-friendly accommodation in the

trendy Moda district. With clean and comfortable rooms, it's an ideal choice for those seeking affordability without compromising on location. Enjoy the local cafes, parks, and the relaxed atmosphere of Kadikoy.

- Cost: Starting from $50 per night

4. Airbnb - Local Living: Authentic Experiences

Charming Istanbul Apartment in Beyoglu

- Location: Beyoglu
- Overview: This centrally located Airbnb apartment offers a cozy retreat in the lively Beyoglu district. Experience local living with modern amenities and proximity to cultural hotspots like Galata Tower and Istiklal Avenue.
- Cost: Starting from $80 per night

Bosphorus View Penthouse in Besiktas

- Location: Besiktas

- Overview: For a unique stay, consider this Airbnb penthouse with panoramic views of the Bosphorus. Enjoy the vibrant Besiktas neighborhood and explore local markets, cafes, and the nearby Dolmabahce Palace.
- Cost: Starting from $150 per night

Hotel Recommendations

Certainly! Here are some hotel recommendations in Istanbul across different neighborhoods, each offering a unique experience:

1. Sultanahmet - Historic Charm:

1. Four Seasons Hotel Istanbul at Sultanahmet
   - Location: Sultanahmet Square
   - Overview: Immerse yourself in luxury at this historic hotel, a former prison turned into an elegant sanctuary. With breathtaking views of Hagia Sophia and the Blue Mosque, this Five-Star hotel offers opulent rooms, a tranquil courtyard, and exceptional service. A perfect blend of Ottoman architecture and modern amenities.
   - Cost: Starting from $500 per night
2. Hotel Amira Istanbul
   - Location: Kucuk Ayasofya Cad. 47, Sultanahmet
   - Overview: Nestled in a quiet corner of Sultanahmet, Hotel Amira Istanbul provides a cozy retreat with a blend of traditional Turkish decor and contemporary comfort. The rooftop terrace offers panoramic views,

and the hotel's warm hospitality ensures a memorable stay.

- Cost: Starting from $150 per night

2. Taksim - Modern Sophistication:

3. Pera Palace Hotel, Jumeirah

- Location: Mesrutiyet Cad. 52-54, Taksim
- Overview: A historic gem, the Pera Palace is a luxury hotel that has hosted royalty and literary legends. The rooms are a blend of timeless elegance and modern amenities. Enjoy the iconic Patisserie de Pera and the atmospheric Orient Bar for a taste of the hotel's storied past.
- Cost: Starting from $300 per night

4. Niles Hotel Istanbul

- Location: Asmalı Mescit, Taksim
- Overview: Niles Hotel combines boutique charm with a central location. This budget-friendly option offers clean and comfortable rooms, making it an ideal choice

for those who want to be in the heart of Taksim without breaking the bank.

- Cost: Starting from $120 per night

3. Kadikoy - Local Vibe:

5. DoubleTree by Hilton Istanbul Moda

- Location: Caferaga Mahallesi, Kadikoy
- Overview: DoubleTree by Hilton in Kadikoy offers modern comfort with a touch of local flair. Enjoy stunning views of the Bosphorus, contemporary design, and a rooftop terrace. With proximity to local attractions, it's an excellent choice for a comfortable stay in Kadikoy.
- Cost: Starting from $150 per night

6. Hush Hostel Lounge

- Location: Caferaga Mahallesi, Kadikoy
- Overview: For budget-conscious travelers, Hush Hostel Lounge in Kadikoy offers a friendly atmosphere and modern amenities. Explore the vibrant Kadikoy district, known

for its markets, street art, and diverse culinary scene.

- Cost: Starting from $30 per night

4. Airbnb - Local Living:

7. Charming Istanbul Apartment in Beyoglu

- Location: Beyoglu
- Overview: Experience local living in this Airbnb apartment situated in the heart of Beyoglu. With its cozy ambiance and proximity to cultural hotspots like Galata Tower and Istiklal Avenue, it provides an authentic Istanbul experience.
- Cost: Starting from $80 per night

8. Bosphorus View Penthouse in Besiktas

- Location: Besiktas
- Overview: For a unique stay, consider this Airbnb penthouse with panoramic views of the Bosphorus. Enjoy the vibrant Besiktas neighborhood and explore local markets, cafes, and the nearby Dolmabahce Palace.

- Cost: Starting from $150 per night

Airbnb and Alternative Accommodations

When planning your stay in Istanbul, consider the diverse range of accommodation options available beyond traditional hotels. From cozy apartments to charming guesthouses, Airbnb and alternative accommodations offer unique experiences that can enhance your visit to the city.

1. Airbnb:

Description: Airbnb provides a platform for booking a wide range of accommodations, including apartments, houses, and even unique stays like rooftop lofts and historic mansions. Hosts often offer personalized touches and local insights to enhance your stay.

Locations: Explore neighborhoods like Sultanahmet, Beyoğlu, and Kadıköy for a variety of

Airbnb listings catering to different preferences and budgets.

Cost: Prices vary depending on the type of accommodation, location, and amenities offered. You can find budget-friendly options as well as luxurious apartments with stunning views of the city.

2. Boutique Hotels:

Description: Boutique hotels in Istanbul offer a blend of personalized service, unique design, and intimate ambiance. Many boutique hotels are housed in historic buildings, providing a glimpse into the city's rich heritage.

Locations: Look for boutique hotels in trendy neighborhoods like Karaköy, Çukurcuma, and Galata for a stylish and memorable stay.

Cost: While boutique hotels may be more expensive than standard hotels, they often provide exceptional value with their attention to detail, personalized service, and distinctive atmosphere.

3. Guesthouses and Pensions:

Description: Guesthouses and pensions offer a cozy and homely atmosphere, perfect for travelers seeking a more intimate experience. These accommodations are often family-run, providing a warm welcome and personalized recommendations.

Locations: Explore neighborhoods like Balat, Fener, and Üsküdar for charming guest houses tucked away in historic districts.

Cost: Guesthouses and pensions typically offer affordable rates compared to hotels, making them an excellent option for budget-conscious travelers seeking a comfortable and authentic stay.

---

4. Serviced Apartments:

Description: Serviced apartments provide the comforts of home with the convenience of hotel amenities. Ideal for longer stays or travelers seeking more space and privacy, serviced apartments offer fully equipped kitchens, living areas, and additional services.

Locations: Look for serviced apartments in central neighborhoods like Şişli, Levent, and Maslak for easy access to shopping, dining, and public transportation.

Cost: Prices for serviced apartments vary depending on the size, location, and amenities provided. They can be a cost-effective option for families or groups traveling together.

5. Hostels and Backpacker Accommodations:

Description: Hostels and backpacker accommodations cater to budget travelers and solo adventurers seeking affordable lodging options. These accommodations often offer dormitory-style rooms, communal areas, and social activities.

Locations: Find hostels in popular neighborhoods like Beyoğlu, Taksim, and Kadıköy, known for their vibrant nightlife and cultural attractions.

Cost: Hostels offer some of the most budget-friendly accommodation options in Istanbul, making them ideal for travelers looking to save money on lodging while connecting with fellow adventurers.

Chapter Three

Navigating Istanbul

Navigating Istanbul: A Continuous Exploration

Welcome to Istanbul, where every street corner tells a tale and every district begs to be discovered. Navigating this bustling city is an essential aspect of your visit, and Istanbul offers a variety of transportation alternatives to ensure a flawless and engaging experience. In this part, we will look at the subtleties of public transit, including the efficient networks that link ancient sites, lively marketplaces, and contemporary neighborhoods. Join us on a voyage through the many types of public transit, guaranteeing that you can easily travel Istanbul and go on an adventure of discovery.

Public Transportation.

Istanbul's public transit system is a dynamic network that links the city's many areas. From ancient trams reverberating through cobblestone alleys to contemporary metro lines crossing both continents, Istanbul's public transit system provides access to immersive experiences.

-Metro

Metro: Navigating Istanbul with Speed and Precision.

Istanbul's metro system is a technological wonder, seamlessly linking vital neighborhoods on the city's European and Asian sides. With its extensive network and modern appearance, the metro is a popular option for both residents and tourists looking for a quick and simple mode of transit.

Key features:

Lines and Connectivity:

Istanbul's metro system consists of multiple lines, including the M1, M2, and M6, each servicing a unique route and neighborhood.

The M1 line links Ataturk Airport with the city center, offering a direct route for flight passengers.

The M2 line runs from Yenikapi to Haciosman, passing through popular neighborhoods such as Taksim Square and Levent.

The M6 line, often known as the Marmaray, connects the European and Asian sides via an underwater tunnel under the Bosphorus.

The metro system in Istanbul is noted for its regularity and effectiveness, making it an excellent alternative for traversing the city's busy environment.

Avoid traffic and get to your destination quickly, giving you more time to experience the city's attractions.

Pricing:

Istanbulkart is a contactless smart card that allows

passengers to utilize public transit, including the metro.

The Istanbulkart may be bought and recharged at a variety of kiosks, making it an affordable choice for hassle-free travel.

The card enables users to switch between means of transportation, such as buses, trams, and ferries, providing flexibility during their trip.

For individuals without an Istanbulkart, single travel tokens are available at metro stations for a slightly higher rate.

Tokens are eligible for one-way trips and must be used within a certain time range following purchase.

Pricing details:

Istanbulkart Initial cost: 10 Turkish Liras (TL) (subject to vary)

Metro Fares with Istanbulkart: Around 3 TL per trip.

The single journey token price is somewhat more

than the Istanbulkart fare.

Tips: Ensure your Istanbulkart has enough credit before using the subway.

Check the Istanbulkart balance at authorized machines or kiosks at metro stations.

Familiarize yourself with metro routes and transfer places to ensure smooth travel across Istanbul.

Accept the speed and accuracy of Istanbul's metro system, where each voyage becomes a chance to effortlessly experience the city's different landscapes. Whether traveling from the airport to the center of Istanbul or moving between renowned neighborhoods, the metro is a dependable companion for a memorable trip.

-Trams

Trams: Nostalgic Journeys through Istanbul's Heritage.

Istanbul's famed trams wind through the city's old streets, offering a nostalgic and beautiful method of transportation. These bright vehicles not only link key sites but also provide passengers with a picturesque ride through some of Istanbul's most attractive areas.

Key features:

Historical Routes:

Trams, notably the T1 line, go through ancient areas, making them an important component of Istanbul's cultural fabric.

The T1 line, commonly known as the "Taksim-Kabatas Tram," links prominent neighborhoods such as Sultanahmet, Eminonu, and Karakoy.

Scenic views:

Enjoy magnificent vistas as trams weave through lively markets, past old mosques, and along the Bosphorus shoreline.

The T1 line, in particular, provides views of prominent monuments like the Hagia Sophia and the Blue Mosque.

Pricing:

Istanbulkart:

Similar to the metro system, the Istanbulkart is the primary mode of payment for tram journeys.

Passengers may use the Istanbulkart to board trams, enabling a smooth and cost-effective ride.

For individuals without an Istanbulkart, single travel tokens are available at tram stops for a slightly higher rate.

Tokens are eligible for one-way trips and must be used within a certain time range following purchase.

Pricing details:

Istanbulkart Initial cost: 10 Turkish Liras (TL) (subject to vary)

Tram fare with Istanbulkart is around 3 TL per trip.

Single Journey Token Fare: Slightly more than Istanbulkart fare.

Practical tips:

Capture the sense of Istanbul's past by taking a

---

tram ride throughout the day or evening, when the city lights up.

Check your Istanbulkart balance before boarding to guarantee smooth travel.

Plan your travel while keeping tram timings in mind, particularly during peak hours.

- Buses

Buses: Versatile Journeys Through Istanbul's Tapestry

In Istanbul's fast-paced environment, buses emerge as the dynamic pulse of public transit. Buses, with their broad network that includes both well-traveled routes and off-the-beaten-path locations, provide an exciting way to explore the city's different neighborhoods and landscapes. Whether you're looking for major sites or hidden jewels, Istanbul's buses offer a voyage that goes beyond transportation, enabling you to immerse yourself in the city's pulsating pulse. Join us on a voyage through the city's tapestry, where each bus ride is an experience in itself.

Key features:

Comprehensive Network:

Istanbul's bus system covers the whole city, connecting neighborhoods, marketplaces, and cultural centers that other modes of transit may not reach.

Passengers can enjoy a full tour of Istanbul thanks to the several bus routes that serve different districts.

Buses are a flexible mode of transportation, serving both famous tourist routes and local commuting.

With multiple bus stations distributed across the city, visitors can easily board and depart.

Pricing:

Istanbulkart:

Istanbulkart, like other forms of public transit, is the primary payment method for bus journeys.

The Istanbulkart allows passengers to effortlessly

board buses, making it a cost-effective and efficient mode of transportation.

For individuals without an Istanbulkart, single travel tokens may be purchased at bus terminals.

Tokens provide one-time usage for a certain route and must be used within a certain time range.

Pricing details:

Istanbulkart's initial cost is 10 Turkish Lira (TL) (subject to change).

Bus fares with Istanbulkart: Around 3 TL per trip.

The single journey token price is somewhat more than the Istanbulkart fare.

Practical tips:

Use real-time transportation applications to monitor bus timetables and routes.

Pay attention to bus numbers and routes to ensure you catch the proper bus for your destination.

Explore Istanbul's different districts and marketplaces by taking a picturesque bus journey and enjoying the native rhythm.

Discover Istanbul's neighborhoods, marketplaces, and cultural hotspots via the adaptable network of buses, where each ride offers not just transportation but also a comprehensive tour of the city's vivid tapestry.

-Taxis and Ride-Sharing

Taxis and Ride-Sharing: Personalized Journeys through Istanbul's Lanes

Taxis and ride-sharing services stand out as the pinnacle of customized travel amid Istanbul's many transportation alternatives. These means of transportation are ideal for people wanting a more private and personalized experience, since they provide convenience, flexibility, and the freedom to explore the city at their leisure. As you negotiate the crowded streets, taxis and ride-sharing services become your chariots, allowing you to effortlessly weave through Istanbul's rich tapestry.

Key features:

Convenience and Door-to-Door Service:

Taxis and ride-sharing services provide door-to-door service, making them perfect for customers who have specified destinations or travel preferences.

Enjoy the ease of being dropped off in your preferred spot, whether it's a historical place, a lively market, or a fashionable area.

Flexibility and Personal Space: These means of transportation provide travelers with individualized and direct routes, enhancing their travel experience.

Enjoy the comfort of a private location, making it a perfect choice for individuals who value solitude on their trips.

Pricing:

Taxis in Istanbul use a metered system. To precisely establish the fee, ensure that the driver activates the meter at the start of your ride.

While cabs are handy, it is necessary to be

---

acquainted with the local currency to prevent misunderstandings during payment.

Ride-Share Services:

Uber operates in Istanbul, adding a layer of convenience and dependability.

Ride-sharing applications provide clear pricing, enabling users to estimate rates before confirming their trips.

Practical tips:

Know Your Route: Provide explicit instructions or utilize navigation tools to lead the driver to your destination, particularly if it is a less well-known region.

Payment: Taxis typically take cash, but ride-sharing services deduct fares automatically from associated payment methods.

Communicate clearly: While language obstacles may exist, a few simple Turkish words or written instructions might help improve communication.

Cost Estimate:

Taxi fare: starting at about 5 TL for the first flag-down and extra expenses every kilometer.

Ride-Sharing Fare: Prices vary depending on distance and demand and are stated transparently on the app.

-**Walking Tours**

Walking Tours: Discovering Istanbul's Charms. Step by step.

Walking excursions in Istanbul's center, where history meets modernity, transform into intimate explorations of the city's essence. These excursions, led by the rhythmic beats of your footsteps, enable you to discover hidden jewels, take in the fragrances of busy marketplaces, and observe the contrast of antique buildings against modern settings. Join us as we lace up our shoes and go across Istanbul's streets, where each step tells a tale.

Key features:

Walking tours in Istanbul provide an immersive experience to learn about the city's culture, history, and local life.

Knowledgeable guides provide insights into the city's rich tapestry, providing anecdotes and stories that bring each location to life.

Flexibility and Personalization: Explore at your own leisure, stopping at interesting places or exploring attractive neighborhoods.

Choose from a variety of walking tours based on diverse topics, such as historical places, gastronomic pleasures, and bright street art.

Popular walking tour routes:

1. Sultanahmet Historic Area: See prominent monuments including Hagia Sophia, the Blue Mosque, and Topkapi Palace.

Wander around Sultanahmet Square, immersing yourself in Istanbul's rich history.

2. Galata and Beyoglu Districts: The Galata Bridge

connects the old and contemporary parts of the city. Stroll along Istiklal Avenue, a busy thoroughfare dotted with stores, cafés, and street performers.

3. Kadikoy Cuisine Tour: Explore the eclectic gastronomic scene of Kadikoy, including local specialties and street cuisine.

Discover the bustling marketplaces and beach promenades of this Asian-side area.

Practical tips:

Comfortable Footwear: Istanbul's streets may be unpredictable, so comfortable walking shoes are necessary for a pleasant visit.

Weather Considerations: Check the weather forecast before planning your walking excursion, taking into account issues such as heat and rain.

Local Guides: Opt for guided walking tours led by experienced locals who can give detailed information and answer questions.

Cost Estimate:

Guided walking tours: Prices vary depending on the

length and subject of the trip, but normally range from $20 to $50 per participant.

Self-Guided Tours: Explore for free by following self-guided tours on maps or apps.

Take a voyage of discovery through Istanbul's charming streets, where each step exposes a new aspect of this fascinating city. Walking tours provide a unique combination of inquiry and connection, enabling you to become a part of the dynamic story that develops with each step.

-Renting Bicycles and Scooters

Renting Bicycles and Scooters: Navigating Istanbul with Two-Wheeled Freedom.

In Istanbul's vibrant tapestry, where old elegance meets contemporary vitality, renting bicycles and scooters emerges as a freeing and environmentally beneficial method to explore the city. With the wind in your hair and the city at your fingertips, these two-wheeled experiences provide a unique view of

Istanbul's streets, enabling you to weave through medieval passageways, cruise along the Bosphorus, and enjoy the freedom of self-guided exploration.

Key features:

Flexibility and speed:

Bicycles and scooters provide a versatile means of transportation, enabling you to easily negotiate tiny streets and avoid traffic.

Enjoy the freedom to ride at your own speed, whether through historic districts or along the seaside.

To reduce environmental impact when exploring the city, consider using bicycles or scooters.

Navigate Istanbul's different landscapes without leaving a carbon imprint, helping to create a greener and cleaner urban environment.

Popular Rental Locations:

1. Sultanahmet and Eminonu are ideal for seeing historical attractions like the Hagia Sophia, Blue Mosque, and Grand Bazaar.

Navigate the Bosphorus while enjoying the magnificent vistas and bustling ambiance of Eminonu Square.

2. Kadikoy and Moda are ideal for exploring the Asian side's bustling districts, beach promenades, and local markets.

Ride around the Kadikoy shoreline and discover Moda, a stylish area.

3. Besiktas and Ortakoy: Explore the European side's colorful areas, including Besiktas' busy markets and Ortakoy's famed shoreline.

Enjoy a trip around the Bosphorus, passing iconic attractions such as the Bosphorus Bridge and Dolmabahce Palace.

Rental Tips:

Safety First: Wear helmets, particularly while riding scooters, and follow traffic laws to ensure a safe voyage.

App-Based Rentals: Use smartphone applications to locate available bicycles or scooters and easily unlock them.

Check the local regulations. For a more enjoyable ride, familiarize yourself with local traffic restrictions and designated bike lanes.

Cost Estimate:

Bicycle rentals typically cost $5 to $15 per hour, with day prices available for prolonged exploration.

Scooter rentals: Prices range from $0.20 to $0.40 per minute, depending on the scooter type and rental platform.

Chapter Four

Must-Visit Attractions

Must-Visit Attractions in Istanbul: A Tapestry of Timeless Wonders

Welcome to Istanbul, a city where the past and

present seamlessly intertwine, creating a tapestry of timeless wonders waiting to be explored. Each cobblestone street, each iconic landmark, and each bustling market tells a story that spans centuries. In this section, we invite you to embark on a journey through Istanbul's must-visit attractions, where history comes alive, and the vibrant spirit of the city unfolds at every turn. Join us as we navigate through the enchanting realms of palaces, mosques, bazaars, and more, unlocking the secrets that make Istanbul a treasure trove of cultural richness.

Iconic Landmarks:

Hagia Sophia

Hagia Sophia: A Divine Symphony of Faith and Architecture

Introduction:

In the heart of Istanbul stands a living testament to the city's rich and diverse history — Hagia Sophia. Originally built as a cathedral in the 6th century, this architectural marvel has witnessed the rise and fall of empires, transitioning from a Byzantine masterpiece to an Ottoman imperial mosque and, finally, a secular museum. Today, Hagia Sophia welcomes visitors as a symbol of unity, bridging the gap between different eras and faiths.

Journey Through Time:

Begin your exploration by entering through the grand entrance, where centuries-old marble floors echo the footsteps of Byzantine emperors. As you ascend to the upper galleries, intricate mosaics depicting religious scenes and celestial figures come into view, each tile whispering stories of devotion and artistic brilliance.

Unique Features:

Marvel at the massive dome, an engineering feat that once stood as the largest in the world. Capture the interplay of light as it filters through centuries-old stained glass windows, creating an ethereal ambiance. Hagia Sophia's minarets and domes, standing side by side, showcase the harmonious coexistence of different cultural and religious influences.

Practical Information:

- Location: Sultanahmet Square
- How to Get There: Accessible by tram and metro. The Sultanahmet tram station is just a brief stroll from here..
- Opening Hours: Check official schedules, as Hagia Sophia may have special visiting hours.

Blue Mosque

Blue Mosque (Sultan Ahmed Mosque): A Symphony of Blue and Faith

Introduction:

Nestled beside Hagia Sophia, the Blue Mosque, or Sultan Ahmed Mosque, paints the skyline of Istanbul with its six minarets and cascading domes. Commissioned in the 17th century, this mosque is a harmonious blend of Ottoman and Byzantine architectural influences, earning its nickname from the stunning blue tiles adorning its interior.

Journey Through Faith and Art:

Step into the expansive courtyard, where the grandeur of the mosque unfolds. As you enter, gaze upon the intricate blue tiles that cover the interior, creating an awe-inspiring atmosphere. The central dome and semi-domes, supported by elegant columns, form a celestial canopy that beckons visitors to contemplate the divine.

Unique Features:

Explore the mosque's interior adorned with over 20,000 handmade ceramic tiles, each contributing to the intricate floral patterns and calligraphy. The mihrab, a masterpiece of marble and tile, guides the faithful in prayer. Witness the interplay of natural light through the numerous windows, casting a serene glow over the prayer hall.

Practical Information:

- Location: Sultanahmet Square

- How to Get There: Accessible on foot from Hagia Sophia and Sultanahmet Tram Station.
- Visiting Hours: Open to visitors outside of prayer times.

Topkapi Palace

Topkapi Palace: Unveiling Ottoman Grandeur and Intrigue

Introduction:

At the crossroads of history and opulence stands Topkapi Palace, a sprawling complex that once served as the epicenter of Ottoman imperial power. Overlooking the Bosphorus, this palace holds within its walls a treasure trove of artifacts, from imperial thrones to sacred relics, offering a glimpse into the lavish lifestyle of Ottoman sultans.

Journey Through Imperial Splendor:

Embark on a journey through the palace gates, where meticulously landscaped gardens greet you. Wander through ornate chambers adorned with gilded decorations and exquisite tiles. The Harem, a private world within the palace, whispers tales of intrigue and royal secrets.

Unique Features:

Marvel at the dazzling collections within the palace, including the Spoonmaker's Diamond and the Topkapi Dagger. Stand in awe of the panoramic views from the terraces, where the Bosphorus unfolds beneath, connecting Europe and Asia. The

---

Imperial Council Chamber echoes with the decisions that shaped empires.

Practical Information:

- Location: Sultanahmet Square
- How to Get There: Walking distance from Hagia Sophia and Blue Mosque.
- Entrance Fee: Check official websites for up-to-date ticket prices.

Grand Bazaar

Grand Bazaar: A Labyrinth of Treasures in Istanbul's Heart

Introduction:

Step into the vibrant heart of Istanbul's commerce, where history and trade converge – the Grand Bazaar. Dating back to the 15th century, this bustling market stands as one of the world's oldest and largest covered markets, offering a sensory journey through labyrinthine alleys adorned with dazzling treasures and the echoes of centuries-old commerce.

Journey Through Time:

Enter through one of the grand gates, and you'll find yourself transported to a world where the past intertwines with the present. The Grand Bazaar has been a hub of trade and cultural exchange for generations, creating an atmosphere that resonates with the voices of merchants and the footsteps of eager shoppers.

Unique Features:

Explore the kaleidoscope of colors and scents as you navigate through over 4,000 shops, each offering a myriad of goods. From intricately woven carpets to gleaming jewelry, fragrant spices to traditional textiles, the Grand Bazaar is a treasure trove that reflects the rich tapestry of Turkish craftsmanship.

Journey Through the Bazaar:

1. Main Avenues: Begin your exploration along the bustling main avenues, where shops

showcase an array of Turkish delights, ceramics, and textiles. The dynamic energy of the market surrounds you, inviting you to immerse yourself in the vibrant atmosphere.

2. Copper Bazaar: Navigate towards the Copper Bazaar, where the gleam of handcrafted copperware captures the eye. Marvel at the skill of artisans as they meticulously shape and adorn each piece, creating a symphony of craftsmanship.

3. Spice Market: Venture into the Spice Market within the Grand Bazaar, where the air is infused with the intoxicating aromas of spices, herbs, and teas. Engage your senses as you explore stalls filled with vibrant colors and exotic fragrances.

4. Jewelry Section: Lose yourself in the Jewelry Section, where intricate designs and precious gemstones beckon. From traditional Turkish pieces to modern creations, this section is a

testament to the enduring allure of Turkish craftsmanship.

Practical Information:

- Location: Beyazıt, close to Sultanahmet Square
- How to Get There: Accessible by tram, with the Beyazıt-Kapalıçarşı tram stop conveniently located.
- Opening Hours: Typically open from morning until late afternoon, but individual shop hours may vary.

Spice Bazaar

Spice Bazaar: A Fragrant Tapestry of Istanbul's Culinary   Heritage

Introduction:

Step into the aromatic embrace of Istanbul's culinary soul, where centuries of spice trade and vibrant flavors converge – the Spice Bazaar. Also known as the Egyptian Bazaar, this enchanting market, dating back to the 17th century, is a sensory celebration of spices, herbs, teas, and delectable Turkish delights. Immerse yourself in the fragrant tapestry that weaves through its historic corridors.

Journey Through Aromas:

Enter through the grand gateways, and the air immediately becomes infused with a symphony of aromas. The Spice Bazaar beckons you to explore its myriad stalls, each laden with colorful pyramids of spices and the promise of culinary delights. As you navigate the bustling alleys, the rhythmic chants of vendors and the rustle of spice-filled sacks create a vibrant atmosphere.

Unique Features:

Dive into a world where spices are more than ingredients; they're a cultural heritage. From the fiery kick of Turkish red pepper (pul biber) to the sweet aroma of saffron, the Spice Bazaar offers a kaleidoscope of flavors that have tantalized palates for generations. Beyond spices, discover an array of teas, dried fruits, nuts, and traditional Turkish sweets.

Journey Through Bazaar

1. Spicee Stalls: Begin your exploration at the spice stalls, where mounds of vivid spices create a visual feast. Engage with vendors who share the stories behind each spice, offering insights into their culinary uses and cultural significance.

2. Tea Shops: Adjacent to the spice stalls, you'll find tea shops adorned with colorful tea canisters. Sip on traditional Turkish tea as you absorb the lively ambiance and plan your culinary adventure.

3. Turkish Delights: Indulge your sweet tooth with a visit to stalls offering an array of Turkish delights. These delectable confections, infused with flavors like rose, pomegranate, and mint, provide a delightful contrast to the savory world of spices.

4. Dried Fruits and Nuts: Explore sections dedicated to dried fruits and nuts, where apricots, figs, pistachios, and more await.

The vibrant colors and natural sweetness create a feast for the eyes and palate.

Practical Information:

- Location: Eminönü, near the Galata Bridge
- How to Get There: Easily accessible by tram, with the Eminönü tram stop nearby.
- Opening Hours: Typically open from morning until late afternoon, but individual shop hours may vary.

Bosphorus Cruise

Bosphorus Cruise: Navigating Istanbul's Maritime Symphony

Introduction:

Embark on a maritime odyssey that transcends time and connects continents – the Bosphorus Cruise. Istanbul's iconic waterway, the Bosphorus Strait, is a natural masterpiece that weaves through the city, separating Europe from Asia. A Bosphorus Cruise is not just a boat ride; it's a mesmerizing journey that unveils panoramic views, historic landmarks, and the enchanting fusion of East and West.

Journey Through Maritime Splendor:

As you step aboard the cruise vessel, feel the gentle sway beneath your feet and the invigorating breeze whispering tales of seafaring adventures. The Bosphorus Cruise promises a front-row seat to Istanbul's maritime symphony, where centuries of history unfold against the picturesque backdrop of palaces, mosques, and waterfront mansions.

Unique Features:

Navigate along the waterway that has been the lifeblood of Istanbul for centuries. Marvel at the architectural marvels lining the shores, from Ottoman palaces to modern residences. The Bosphorus, adorned with boats of varying sizes, reflects the vibrant energy of a city where East meets West.

Journey Through the Cruise:

1. Golden Horn: Depart from the Eminönü or Karaköy docks, passing through the Golden Horn, where the city's historic districts unfold. Admire the Galata Tower and the vibrant neighborhoods that hug the shoreline.

2. Rumeli Fortress: Cruise past the formidable Rumeli Fortress, a medieval stronghold that once guarded the Bosphorus. Marvel at its imposing walls and envision the strategic importance it held in centuries past.

3. Bosphorus Bridges: Sail beneath the Bosphorus Bridges, linking Europe and Asia. The sight of these engineering marvels, especially the illuminated bridges at night, adds a touch of modernity to the timeless beauty of the strait.

4. Dolmabahce Palace: Admire the opulence of Dolmabahce Palace from the water, its majestic facade and ornate details creating a

breathtaking panorama. Revel in the contrast between the historic architecture and the contemporary energy of the city.

Practical Information:

- Departure Points: Various docks including Eminönü and Kabataş.
- Duration: Cruises typically last 1.5 to 2 hours.
- Options: Daytime and evening cruises available, each offering a unique perspective of Istanbul.

Basilica Cistern

Basilica Cistern: Subterranean Marvel of Istanbul's Ancient Elegance

Introduction:

Beneath the bustling streets of Istanbul lies a hidden world of ancient marvels – the Basilica Cistern. Built in the 6th century during the Byzantine era, this subterranean reservoir is a captivating testament to Istanbul's architectural prowess and the ability to turn necessity into art. Step into the cool embrace of the Basilica Cistern, where columns rise from water, and history whispers in every echoing droplet.

Journey Through Subterranean Tranquility: Descend into the dimly lit entrance, and a surreal world awaits beneath the city's surface. The Basilica Cistern is an engineering marvel, a vast underground chamber supported by a forest of columns, creating an otherworldly atmosphere that transports you to a time when Istanbul was still Constantinople.

Unique Features:

Marvel at the sheer size of the cistern, which once stored water for the Great Palace of Constantinople. The two Medusa heads, used as column bases, add an air of mystery to the space. The soft illumination reflects off the water's surface, creating a tranquil ambiance that contrasts with the vibrant energy above ground.

Journey Through the Cistern:

1. The Forest of Columns: Enter the cistern to witness the forest of 336 columns, each rising from the water to support the massive

brick vaults. The symmetry and precision of the columns evoke a sense of awe and wonder.

2. Medusa Heads: Discover the two Medusa heads, one upside down and the other on its side, used as column bases. The origin and purpose of these ancient artifacts remain shrouded in mystery, adding an intriguing layer to the cistern's history.

3. The Hen's Eye Pillar: Seek out the Hen's Eye Pillar, where a tear-shaped stain on one of the columns is believed to have healing properties. Visitors often touch the stain, seeking a connection to the cistern's mystical aura.

Practical Information:

- Location: Yerebatan Cad. 13, Sultanahmet Square
- How to Get There: Walking distance from Hagia Sophia and the Blue Mosque.

- Opening Hours: Check official schedules, as operating hours may vary.

Galata Tower

Galata Tower: A Timeless Beacon Overlooking Istanbul's Splendor

Introduction:

Piercing the skyline with timeless grace, the Galata Tower stands as a sentinel, offering panoramic views of Istanbul's enchanting cityscape. Dating back to the medieval era, this architectural gem has witnessed the rise and fall of empires, evolving from a medieval watchtower to a panoramic observatory that beckons visitors to ascend and behold the breathtaking   vistas   that   unfold   beneath.

Journey Through the Tower's History:

Ascend the narrow streets of the Galata district to reach the base of the tower, where medieval stone meets contemporary curiosity. The Galata Tower, initially constructed in the 14th century, has served various purposes over the centuries, including as an observation point for spotting fires and as an astronomical observatory.

Unique Features:

Marvel at the cylindrical structure crowned with a conical roof, showcasing a blend of medieval and Ottoman architectural influences. As you ascend, the tower reveals its lattice of windows, each offering a framed view of Istanbul that transcends time. Whether bathed in the golden hues of sunrise or aglow under the city lights, the Galata Tower is a timeless emblem.

Journey Through the Tower:

1. Observation Deck: Reach the top of the tower to the observation deck, where Istanbul unveils itself in a 360-degree panorama. The Bosphorus Strait, Golden Horn, and iconic landmarks like Hagia Sophia and Topkapi Palace paint an awe-inspiring tableau.

2. Historical Exhibits: Explore the interior of the tower, where historical exhibits narrate its diverse past. The Galata Tower has been a

military outpost, a prison, and an observatory, each chapter leaving its mark on the stone walls.

3. Café and Restaurant: Indulge in a moment of relaxation at the café and restaurant situated on the upper levels. Savor Turkish delights or a cup of Turkish coffee while basking in the mesmerizing views.

Practical Information:

- Location: Galata Kulesi, Beyoğlu
- How to Get There: Accessible by foot from the Galata Bridge or via public transportation. A leisurely stroll across the Galata Bridge adds to the experience.
- Entrance Fee: Check official websites for up-to-date ticket prices.

Istiklal Avenue

Istiklal Avenue: Istanbul's Vibrant Artery of Culture and   Commerce

Introduction:

Step onto the bustling stage of Istanbul's cosmopolitan life, where history, culture, and commerce converge – Istiklal Avenue. This lively and iconic street, stretching for over a mile through the heart of Beyoğlu, is a sensory celebration that pulses with the rhythm of the city. Istiklal Avenue is not merely a thoroughfare; it's a living boulevard that invites you to explore its vibrant tapestry of shops, cafes, theaters, and the palpable energy of Istanbul's modern spirit.

Journey Through the Boulevard's History:

Begin your journey at Taksim Square, where Istiklal Avenue commences its lively course. The avenue, once known as the Grand Rue de Péra during the Ottoman era, has evolved over time, witnessing the transformations of Istanbul into the dynamic metropolis it is today.

Unique Features:

Stroll along Istiklal Avenue, and you'll find a kaleidoscope of architectural styles, from elegant 19th-century buildings to contemporary storefronts. The nostalgic red tramway adds a touch of charm as it weaves through the bustling crowd, creating a visual symphony of past and present.

Journey Through the Avenue:

1. Shopfronts and Boutiques: Explore the diverse range of shops lining the avenue,

---

where global brands coexist with local boutiques. From high-end fashion to traditional Turkish goods, Istiklal Avenue is a shopper's paradise.

2. Street Performers and Cafes: Immerse yourself in the vibrant street life, where talented musicians, lively street performers, and alfresco cafes create an atmosphere that encourages spontaneous moments of joy. The historic Çiçek Pasajı (Flower Passage) is a must-visit for its nostalgic ambiance and culinary delights.

3. Galatasaray Square: Reach Galatasaray Square, a cultural hub where the historic Galatasaray High School stands proudly. This square is a meeting point for locals, offering a glimpse into Istanbul's intellectual and artistic circles.

Practical Information:

- Location: Beyoğlu, connecting Taksim Square to Galatasaray Square
- How to Get There: Accessible by foot from Taksim Square or via the nostalgic tramway. The historic Tunnel, one of the world's oldest subways, connects the lower and upper sections of the avenue.

Chapter Five

Culinary Delights

Culinary Delights: Local Dishes to Try in Istanbul

Indulging in Istanbul's gastronomic tapestry is a

sensory trip via delicacies that reflect the story of a rich cultural history. Each meal, savory or sweet, is a masterpiece that embodies the city's many influences. Here are some local foods that every keen palate should try:

1. Kebabs: Grilled Delight for the Senses.

Savor the juicy kebabs served at Istanbul's countless restaurants for a true sense of the city. Visit Tarihi Karadeniz Döner for a culinary journey. This legendary eatery, nestled away in the heart of Beyoğlu, is known for its juicy kebabs. The wonderfully seasoned beef, slow-cooked on a vertical rotisserie, melts on your tongue. Prices vary between 20 and 50 Turkish Lira per kebab, making it an inexpensive treat. The mix of spices, the suppleness of the meat, and the pure scent make this culinary masterpiece a real treat for your taste

buds.

2. Baklava: The Sweet Symphony of Layers and Honey

Baklava, a famous Turkish dish, can satisfy your sweet desires. Visit

Karaköy Güllüoğlu, a historic bakery known for its delicious baklava since 1871. This family-owned business has mastered the technique of stacking thin sheets of pastry, filling them with pistachios or walnuts, and drizzling them with honey. A dish of baklava here costs between 10 and 30 Turkish Lira, depending on the variation. The combination of crunchy layers, rich nuts, and sweet honey results in a dessert experience that is nothing short of divine.

3. Meze platter: A feast of little delights.

Embark on a gastronomic trip by savoring Istanbul's varied

tastes with a Meze platter. Meze by Lemon Tree in the fashionable Karaköy area offers a wide variety of choices. This gourmet treat serves a variety of tiny foods, such as hummus, grilled octopus, and filled grape leaves. A meze platter for two costs around 100 to 150 Turkish lira. The freshness of the ingredients, along with the variety of tastes, make it an excellent option for anyone looking to sample the city's culinary offerings in one sitting.

4. Turkish Delight (Lokum), Sweet Confections with a Twist

Explore the world of Turkish delight, also known as Lokum, for a delicious delight with a centuries-long history.

Visit the ancient Haci Bekir, a confectionary institution that has been in operation since 1777. Their Lokum collection, which includes tastes like rose, pomegranate, and mint, demonstrates the skill of Turkish sweets. A box of Turkish Delight normally costs between 20 and 50 Turkish Lira, making it a great keepsake or snack to take on the road. Each piece has the ideal blend of chewiness and sweetness, transporting you to a realm of delight.

5. Balık Ekmek: Fish Sandwich by the Bosphorus.

Enjoy Istanbul's marine spirit with Balık Ekmek, a fish sandwich that embodies the essence of the Bosphorus. Head to the Eminönü shoreline and look for the lively booths that line the Galata Bridge. A Balık Ekmek sandwich with grilled fish, lettuce, and onions costs around 15–25 Turkish Lira. The smokey scent and exquisite flavor combination capture Istanbul's coastline charm. Enjoy your sandwich with a panoramic view of the Bosphorus for an unforgettable gastronomic experience.

Best Restaurants and Street Food in Istanbul

Embark on a culinary journey through Istanbul, where the blend of traditional flavors and contemporary innovation awaits at every turn. Discover the best restaurants and street food vendors that tantalize the taste buds and showcase the city's vibrant gastronomic scene.

**1. Mikla Restaurant: Elevating Turkish Cuisine to New Heights

---

Location: Meşrutiyet Caddesi No.15, Beyoğlu

Opening Hours: Daily, 6:30 PM - 12:00 AM

Overview: Perched atop the Marmara Pera Hotel, Mikla Restaurant offers a panoramic view of Istanbul's skyline. Renowned chef Mehmet Gürs curates a menu that reinterprets traditional Turkish dishes with a modern twist. From lamb shawarma with pistachios to fermented black garlic kebabs, each dish is a culinary masterpiece. The chic ambiance and innovative flavors make Mikla a must-visit for those seeking a refined Turkish dining experience.

2. Çiya Sofrası: A Culinary Exploration of Anatolian Tastes

Location: Caferağa Mahallesi, Güneşlibahçe Sk. No:43, Kadıköy

This is the Opening Hours: Daily, 12:00 PM - 10:00 PM

Overview: Çiya Sofrası in Kadıköy is a gastronomic haven, showcasing the rich tapestry of Anatolian cuisine. The restaurant, led by chef Musa Dağdeviren, sources ingredients from across Turkey to create an extensive menu. From kebabs to mezes, each dish is a tribute to the diverse regional flavors. The rustic charm of the restaurant and the commitment to authentic tastes make Çiya Sofrası a beloved destination for locals and tourists alike.

**3. Karaköy Güllüoğlu: The Epitome of Baklava Bliss

Location: Rıhtım Caddesi Katlı Otopark Altı No:3, Karaköy

This is the Opening Hours: Daily, 8:00 AM - 11:00 PM

Overview: For a sweet interlude, Karaköy Güllüoğlu stands as an institution in the world of baklava. Established in 1871, this family-owned bakery is celebrated for its mastery in crafting the finest layers of pastry filled with pistachios and walnuts. The golden-brown delights, soaked in honey, offer a symphony of flavors. Whether enjoyed on-site or as a take-away treat, Karaköy Güllüoğlu is a sweet haven for dessert enthusiasts.

**4. Süleymaniye Kebapçısı: A Kebab Haven in the Heart of Istanbul

Location: Süleymaniye Mahallesi, İstanbul Üniversitesi Karşısı No:1, Fatih

This is the Opening Hours: Daily, 10:00 AM - 11:00 PM

Overview: Nestled near the historic Süleymaniye Mosque, Süleymaniye Kebapçısı beckons with the irresistible aroma of grilled kebabs. This unassuming gem is praised for its mastery in preparing traditional Turkish kebabs, from Adana to Urfa varieties. The succulent meat, perfectly seasoned and grilled to perfection, offers a culinary delight that captures the essence of authentic Turkish street food.

**5. Balıkçı Sabahattin: Seafood Extravaganza by the Bosphorus

Location: Seyit Hasan Kuyu Sokak No:1, Eminönü

This is the Opening Hours: Daily, 12:00 PM - 11:00 PM

Overview: Embrace the flavors of the Bosphorus at Balıkçı Sabahattin, an iconic seafood restaurant tucked away in Eminönü. With a history dating back to 1947, this culinary institution invites patrons to savor the freshest catch from the sea. From grilled octopus to pan-seared sea bass, each dish showcases the maritime bounty. The nautical-themed décor and the waterfront location make Balıkçı Sabahattin a quintessential destination for seafood enthusiasts.

Turkish Tea and Coffee Culture

Turkish tea and coffee culture is a rich tapestry of tradition and flavor.

Exploring the complicated traditions and delicious tastes of Turkish tea and coffee will transport you to the heart of Turkish hospitality. From the busy streets to the tranquil nooks of traditional teahouses, each sip provides insight into Turkey's cultural fabric and social scene.

**1. Turkish Tea (Çay): Enjoy, Savor, and Socialize.

Tea is more than a beverage in Turkey; it is a cultural tradition that promotes companionship and discourse. The classic tulip-shaped glasses are filled with çay, which may be served strong and black or light and sweet. Visit Çorlulu Ali Paşa Medresesi in the Grand Bazaar to learn about tea-drinking traditions in a historical context. The aromatic drink is often accompanied by vibrant conversations, resulting in a social atmosphere that spans generations. Whether in a crowded tea garden or a private nook of a teahouse, Turkish tea encourages you to stay, converse, and enjoy the simple delight of shared experiences.

**2. Turkish Coffee: An Ancient Brew and Timeless Ritual

Turkish coffee is more than simply a pick-me-up; it

is a centuries-old tradition rich in meaning and taste. The finely ground coffee, water, and sugar (optional) are carefully boiled in a special pot known as a cezve, yielding a velvety, unfiltered beverage. At Mandabatmaz in Beyoğlu, learn the technique of making Turkish coffee in an ambient atmosphere. The fortune-telling process using leftover coffee grounds adds a fascinating element to the experience. Turkish coffee is more than just caffeine; it's a personal journey through history, custom, and the rich tastes that distinguish Turkish coffee culture.

**3. Tea Gardens on the Bosphorus: Scenic Sips with a View

Visit one of the tea gardens along the Bosphorus for a really lovely tea experience. Küçükiftlik Park Tea Garden offers a picturesque view of the Bosphorus Bridge and abundant flora, making it a hidden treasure. The relaxing strains of Turkish classical music, the rustling of leaves, and the mild air create an excellent atmosphere for tea lovers. Whether you like classic black tea or herbal infusions, the tea gardens along the Bosphorus provide a peaceful respite from the city, enabling you to immerse yourself in the splendor of Turkish tea culture.

**4. Historic Coffeehouses: A Glance into the Past.

Visit one of Istanbul's old coffeehouses, where time seems to have stopped. Gülhane Sark Kahvesi, located in the center of the Old City and dating back to the 17th century, appeals with its nostalgic atmosphere. The perfume of freshly ground coffee combines with the sounds of centuries-old conversations. Sip on a cup of Turkish coffee while surrounded by elaborate tiles and classic décor, and you'll be transported to a time when coffee was more than just a beverage; it was an intellectual endeavor.

**5. Spice Bazaar Tea Shops: A Symphony of Aromas.

Navigate the Spice Bazaar's bright aisles to find tea

stores that provide an olfactory trip through Turkish tea flavors. Explore Malatya Pazari Çaycısı's colorful and fragrant teas flavored with spices, fruits, and herbs. The bazaar's hectic environment heightens the encounter, making it a sensory journey. From apple tea to the rejuvenating sage mix, these tea stores capture the variegated and fragrant character of Turkish tea culture.

Whether you're in a crowded tea garden, a historic coffeehouse, or a tiny nook of the Spice Bazaar, Turkish tea and coffee culture encourages you to enjoy the moment. Each cup tells a narrative, connects people, and provides a taste of the warm hospitality that distinguishes Turkish culture.

Chapter Six

Grand Bazaar Shopping Guide.

Begin your shopping adventure in Istanbul,

where the Grand Bazaar serves as a labyrinthine treasure trove, beckoning you to explore its vivid booths and immerse yourself in the rich tapestry of Turkish workmanship. From exquisite carpets to glittering lanterns, every corner of the Grand Bazaar promises one-of-a-kind discoveries and cultural experiences.

**1. Navigating the Grand Bazaar: A Maze of Wonders.

Prepare to be amazed as you enter the Grand Bazaar, one of the world's oldest and biggest covered marketplaces. Located in the center of the

Old City, the bazaar's convoluted lanes host nearly 4,000 stores, providing an authentic shopping experience. Begin your adventure at the Nuruosmaniye Gate, where you will experience the bazaar's enchanting atmosphere.

**2. Carpets and Kilims: Traditional Turkish Elegance.

Wander through the carpet-draped aisles of the Grand Bazaar, where Turkish carpets and kilims unfold like brilliant tapestries. Orkide Halı, a respected carpet business, offers a breathtaking assortment of handmade carpets, each expressing a narrative via complex patterns and rich colors. The skilled team will walk you through the carpet weaving process, assisting you in selecting a piece that reflects both your style and background.

**3. Jewelry and Gold: Glittering Treasures of the Bazaar.

Discover the stunning world of Turkish jewelry at Kuyumcu Hakkı Şahbaz. Nestled inside the Grand

Bazaar, this jewelry boutique shows the centuries-old workmanship that has graced Istanbul. From grandiose Ottoman-style pieces to modern designs, the collection reflects the city's rich jewelry legacy. Kuyumcu Hakkı Şahbaz offers a wide range of jewelry options, from classic rings to one-of-a-kind pendants.

**4. Spices and Turkish Delights: A Culinary Journey.

Allow your senses to lead you to the Spice Bazaar inside the Grand Bazaar, where the air is filled with the perfume of exotic spices. Malatya Pazari Çaycısı offers a diverse selection of spices, teas, and Turkish treats. The brilliant colors and seductive fragrances offer an immersive experience, enabling you to choose spices for your kitchen or indulge in sweet delicacies to recreate Istanbul's tastes at home.

**5. Ceramics and Tiles: Artistry in Every Glaze.

Umay Keramik showcases the creativity of Turkish

ceramics and tiles. This store, nestled away in the Grand Bazaar, displays the complex designs and brilliant colors that distinguish Turkish tilework. From beautiful plates to ornamental tiles, each item showcases decades of skill. The courteous craftspeople at Umay Keramik provide insights into the processes required to create these timeless jewels, making your buying experience both instructive and artistically appealing.

**6. Lanterns and Lamps: Illuminating Turkish Craftwork

For a taste of Turkish mysticism, visit the Grand Bazaar's lantern-filled stores. The collection of mosaic lanterns and bright glass lights dangling from every corner at Avanos Lights will captivate you. The artistry of these lit artworks displays a blend of traditional Turkish design and modern aesthetics. Avanos Lamps has an enticing range of standout pieces as well as gentle glows.

**7. Leather Goods: Timeless Elegance in Each

Stitch

Experience the elegance of Turkish leather at Güler Leather. Nestled in the Grand Bazaar, this boutique offers a wonderful range of leather products, ranging from purses to coats, all created with painstaking attention to detail. Güler Leather's silky textures and timeless patterns make it a top choice for anyone looking for a stylish and long-lasting Turkish memento.

**8. Negotiating Tips: Mastering the Art of Haggling.

As you visit the Grand Bazaar, enjoy the custom of bargaining. Sellers anticipate some negotiating, so don't be afraid to participate in pleasant haggling. Begin with a smile, demonstrate genuine curiosity, and be willing to walk away if necessary. Remember that the aim is not just to make a purchase but also to enjoy the transaction.

Navigating the Grand Bazaar is a fascinating excursion through Turkish art and business. Each store, full of treasures and tales, encourages you to experience Istanbul's lively culture while taking home a piece of its rich history. Whether you're looking for complex fabrics, glittering jewels, or scented spices, the Grand Bazaar offers a fascinating shopping experience that spans time and captivates the senses.

Authentic Turkish Souvenirs.

Authentic Turkish Souvenirs: Treasures to Bring Home From Istanbul

Explore genuine Turkish souvenirs that reflect the spirit of Istanbul's lively culture. From delicately carved pottery to timeless linens, each memento reflects Turkish artistry and heritage.

**1. Turkish Ceramics: Timeless Elegance in Every Glaze.

Accept the creativity of Turkish pottery, a symbol of the country's cultural history. Güler Keramik at the Grand Bazaar offers a dazzling collection of hand-painted plates, bowls, and tiles. Each item embodies the elaborate designs and brilliant colors that have graced Turkish houses for ages. Turkish ceramics are a treasured gift because of their intricate workmanship and classic patterns, which capture a bit of Istanbul's creative character.

**2. Evil Eye Talismans: Avoid Negativity with Turkish Charms

Visit Nazar Boncuğu Evi, a boutique known for its famous Evil Eye talismans. These brilliant blue amulets are said to guard against evil spirits and provide good fortune. Adorn your house or loved ones with these meaningful charms, which come in a variety of sizes and patterns. Nazar Boncuğu Evi sells real Evil Eye items, preserving Turkish superstition and tradition.

**3. Turkish Carpets and Kilims: Artistry Woven Into Every Thread

Denizli Kiliç Hali has a range of carpets and kilims that are both exquisite and genuine Turkish. This famous carpet store in the Grand Bazaar displays handmade masterpieces that reflect Turkey's rich textile tradition. Each carpet offers a distinct tale, with complex designs and brilliant colors. Whether you pick a little kilim or a large carpet, you are not only purchasing a floor covering but also a work of Turkish art.

**4. Traditional Turkish Delights: Sweet Memories for Sharing

 Indulge in the exquisite world of Turkish treats and sweets at Haci Bekir, a confectionary establishment founded in 1777. Treat your taste buds to the delicious symphony of lokum (Turkish pleasure) in a variety of flavors, as well as other classic sweets. These delicacies, packaged in elegantly adorned boxes, provide a genuine and delicious gift for sharing Istanbul's delights with friends and family.

**5. Handwoven Turkish Towels: Practical Elegance.

Jennifer's Hamam in the Grand Bazaar sells Turkish towels known as peshtemals, which are ageless and elegant. These lightweight, quick-drying towels are not only functional but also represent Turkish swimming tradition. The company sells a wide variety of peshtemals in brilliant colors and designs, all handmade using traditional methods. These towels are ideal for daily use or as a fashionable accent, and they make an excellent and genuine Turkish memento.

**6. Turkish Coffee Sets: Brewing Traditions at Home

Bring the tradition of Turkish coffee into your

---

house with a beautifully constructed coffee set by Ali Baba Türk Kahvesi. This business, located in the Spice Bazaar, sells a variety of traditional coffee sets, which include a cezve (coffee pot), fincan (cup), and saucer. Choose a pair with elaborate Ottoman motifs or go for a contemporary touch. The coffee sets provide a concrete link to Istanbul's rich coffee tradition.

**7. Turkish Spices and Tea Blends: A Culinary Adventure.

Kurukahveci Mehmet Efendi offers a varied assortment of spices and tea blends to take you on a gourmet adventure. This Spice Bazaar business is well-known for its finely ground Turkish coffee, but it also sells a variety of spices and tea blends that are beautifully packaged. From fragrant Turkish tea to rich spice combinations, these goods provide a true flavor of Istanbul's culinary history.

**8. Turkish Mosaic Lamps: Light Up Your Home with Art

Mosaic Istanbul's mosaic lamps capture the appeal of Turkish aesthetics. These beautifully constructed lights, which come in a variety of forms and sizes, provide a stunning dance of light and color. Each lamp is a one-of-a-kind work of practical art, made using traditional methods. Whether hanging from the ceiling or put on a tabletop, a Turkish mosaic lamp lends a magical touch to any room.

Exploring these real Turkish souvenirs enables you to take a bit of Istanbul's cultural heritage with you. Each piece, rooted in history and creativity, is a tangible remembrance of your tour through the city's lovely streets.

Local Markets and Boutiques

Local Markets and Boutiques: Istanbul's Hidden Gems for Unique Finds

Embark on a discovery of Istanbul's local markets and boutiques, where the city's vibrant spirit and diverse cultural influences converge. From bustling markets that showcase traditional crafts to boutique stores offering contemporary designs, each destination promises a unique shopping experience.

**1. Arasta Bazaar: Timeless Treasures by the Blue Mosque

Location: Sultanahmet, Arasta Çarşısı, Fatih

Opening Hours: Daily, 9:00 AM - 7:00 PM

Overview: Tucked behind the Blue Mosque, Arasta Bazaar is a hidden gem that offers a tranquil shopping experience. The market is adorned with shops selling traditional Turkish handicrafts, carpets, textiles, and ceramics. As you wander through the cobblestone paths, immerse yourself in the rich heritage of Ottoman craftsmanship. From intricate jewelry to handwoven rugs, Arasta Bazaar is a haven for those seeking authentic souvenirs. The serene ambiance and the proximity to historical landmarks make it a must-visit destination for a leisurely shopping spree.

**2. Karaköy Vintage Shops: Nostalgia in Every Corner

Location: Karaköy, Istanbul

Opening Hours: Varies by shop; generally 11:00 AM - 8:00 PM

Overview: Karaköy, a trendy neighborhood, is home to a collection of vintage shops that beckon with nostalgic charm. Dive into the past at shops like Zubizu Vintage and A La Turca Vintage, where you'll find curated collections of clothing, accessories, and decor items from different eras. Whether you're hunting for a unique fashion piece or a retro souvenir, the vintage shops of Karaköy promise a delightful journey through time. The eclectic atmosphere and the artistic flair of the district add an extra layer of allure to your shopping excursion.

**3. Çukurcuma Antique Shops: Time-Tested Elegance

Location: Çukurcuma Caddesi, Beyoğlu

Opening Hours: Varies by shop; generally 11:00 AM - 7:00 PM

Overview: Çukurcuma, known as Istanbul's antique district, is a treasure trove for those with an appreciation for vintage elegance. The narrow streets are lined with antique shops, each housing a curated selection of furniture, art, and collectibles. Explore iconic spots like Aslı Antiques and Hazzo Pulo Pasajı for a journey through time. Whether you're a serious collector or a casual browser, Çukurcuma's antique shops offer a chance to discover the stories embedded in each timeless piece.

**4. Istiklal Avenue Boutiques: Modern Style, Timeless Appeal

Location: Beyoğlu, Istanbul

Opening Hours: Varies by boutique; generally 10:00 AM - 8:00 PM

Overview: Istiklal Avenue, a bustling thoroughfare, is not only a hub for cultural experiences but also a hotspot for contemporary fashion. Explore boutiques like Armaggan and Mudo Concept, where modern Turkish designers showcase their creations. From stylish clothing to unique accessories, Istiklal Avenue's boutiques cater to diverse tastes. The avenue's lively atmosphere and the fusion of modern and traditional elements create a shopping ambiance that mirrors Istanbul's dynamic spirit.

**5. Gülizar Ottoman Boutique: Turkish Elegance Redefined

Location: Alemdar Mahallesi, Divan Yolu Cad. No:20, Sultanahmet

Opening Hours: Daily, 9:00 AM - 8:00 PM

Overview: Gülizar Ottoman Boutique, nestled in the heart of Sultanahmet, is a haven for those seeking refined Turkish elegance. The boutique offers a curated selection of clothing, accessories, and home decor inspired by Ottoman motifs. Each piece reflects a harmonious blend of traditional craftsmanship and contemporary design. Whether you're in search of a unique fashion statement or an exquisite home accent, Gülizar Ottoman Boutique encapsulates the sophistication and cultural richness of Turkish style.

**6. Feriköy Antika Pazarı: Antiques Amidst Urban Charm

Istanbul Travel Guide 2024

Location: Feriköy Antika Pazarı, Şişli

Opening Hours: Weekends, 10:00 AM - 7:00 PM

Overview: Feriköy Antika Pazarı, a weekend antique market, unfolds in the trendy Şişli district. This open-air market brings together a diverse array of antique dealers offering furniture, jewelry, and curiosities. Whether you're a seasoned collector or a casual browser, the market's laid-back atmosphere and the eclectic mix of treasures create an enjoyable shopping experience. Feriköy Antika Pazarı is a testament to Istanbul's ability to blend the old with the new, providing a glimpse into the city's ever-evolving charm.

Navigate these local markets and boutiques to uncover the hidden gems that define Istanbul's distinctive character. Each destination, whether rooted in tradition or embracing contemporary trends, invites you to partake in the city's dynamic and diverse shopping scene.

Chapter Seven

Nightlife

Nightlife in Istanbul: Bars and Pubs for Memorable Evenings

Discover the vibrant nightlife of Istanbul by exploring its eclectic array of bars and pubs. From rooftop lounges with panoramic views to cozy pubs exuding local charm, each venue offers a unique atmosphere for a night out in this dynamic city.

**1. 360 Istanbul: Rooftop Elegance Overlooking the Bosphorus

Location: Istiklal Caddesi Mısır Apartmanı Kat: 8, Beyoğlu

This is the Opening Hours: Daily, 5:00 PM - 2:00 AM

Overview: Perched atop a historic building on Istiklal Avenue, 360 Istanbul boasts breathtaking panoramic views of the city and the Bosphorus. This rooftop lounge seamlessly transitions from a chic restaurant to a lively bar as the night progresses. With a diverse menu of cocktails and a sophisticated ambiance, 360 Istanbul is a perfect spot for a memorable evening. The contemporary design and the vibrant energy make it a favorite among locals and visitors alike.

**2. Karaköy Güverte: Waterside Charm and Trendy Vibes

Location: Kemankeş Karamustafa Paşa, Istanbul

Opening Hours: Daily, 12:00 PM - 2:00 AM

Overview: Nestled along the shores of the Golden Horn, Karaköy Güverte offers a laid-back yet stylish setting for an evening by the water. With its relaxed atmosphere and trendy decor, this waterside venue is perfect for enjoying a variety of drinks, from classic cocktails to local favorites. Whether you choose a seat on the terrace or opt for the cozy indoor space, Karaköy Güverte provides a delightful escape from the hustle and bustle of the city.

**3. Babylon Bomonti: Music-Fueled Nights in a Cultural Hub

Location: Bomontiada, Tarihi Bomonti Bira Fabrikası, Istanbul

Opening Hours: Events-based; check the schedule

Overview: Babylon Bomonti, housed in the historic Bomonti Beer Factory, is not just a bar but a cultural hub that comes alive with live music performances and DJ sets. The venue hosts an array of events, ranging

---

from jazz nights to electronic beats, creating a dynamic and immersive nightlife experience. With its industrial-chic design and diverse musical offerings, Babylon Bomonti is a must-visit for those seeking a fusion of art, culture, and nightlife in the heart of Istanbul.

**4. Dubh Linn Irish Pub: Cozy Retreat with Irish Hospitality

Location: Asmalımescit Mahallesi, Asmalımescit Cd. No:9, Beyoğlu

Opening Hours: Daily, 2:00 PM - 2:00 AM

Overview: For a taste of Irish hospitality in the heart of Istanbul, Dubh Linn Irish Pub beckons with its warm and welcoming atmosphere. This cozy retreat, adorned with traditional Irish decor, offers a selection of beers, whiskeys, and pub grub. Whether you're looking for a relaxed evening with friends or a lively night with live music, Dubh Linn provides a laid-back yet spirited setting to unwind and enjoy the camaraderie of a classic Irish pub.

**5. Leb-i Derya: Stylish Rooftop Oasis in Beyoğlu

Location: Kumbaracı Yokuşu, No: 57/6, Beyoğlu

Opening Hours: Daily, 12:00 PM - 2:00 AM

Overview: Situated in the heart of Beyoğlu, Leb-i Derya offers a stylish rooftop oasis with panoramic views of the city. This upscale venue is known for its chic ambiance, innovative cocktails, and a menu featuring a fusion of Turkish and Mediterranean flavors. As the evening unfolds, Leb-i Derya transforms into a sophisticated lounge where you can savor culinary delights and enjoy signature cocktails against the backdrop of Istanbul's illuminated skyline.

**6. Unter: Electronica Haven in the Heart of Istanbul

Location: Kumbaracı Yokuşu No: 57, Beyoğlu

Opening Hours: Daily, 6:00 PM - 2:00 AM

Overview: Unter, nestled in the vibrant neighborhood of Beyoğlu, stands out as a haven for electronic music enthusiasts. With its minimalist yet energetic ambiance, Unter attracts a diverse crowd seeking an immersive experience with cutting-edge beats. The venue hosts both local and international DJs, creating a dynamic atmosphere that resonates with Istanbul's progressive nightlife scene. Whether you're a dedicated electronic

---

music fan or a casual explorer, Unter promises a memorable night out in the heart of the city.

Embark on a nightlife adventure in Istanbul, where these bars and pubs offer an eclectic mix of atmospheres and experiences. From trendy rooftops to waterside retreats, each venue invites you to savor the dynamic energy and diverse cultural influences that define Istanbul's vibrant after-dark scene.

Nightclubs

Nightlife in Istanbul: Dance the Night Away at Exclusive Nightclubs

Experience the pulsating rhythm of Istanbul's nightlife by exploring its vibrant array of nightclubs. From glamorous venues with renowned DJs to intimate spaces offering eclectic beats, each nightclub promises an unforgettable evening of music and dance.

**1. Reina: Glamorous Riverside Haven

Location: Muallim Naci Caddesi No:44, Ortaköy

Opening Hours: Varies by event; typically opens late evening

Overview: Positioned along the Bosphorus, Reina stands as one of Istanbul's most iconic and glamorous nightclubs. This upscale venue features multiple dance floors, chic lounges, and a breathtaking outdoor terrace with panoramic views. Renowned for hosting international DJs and celebrities, Reina delivers an opulent nightlife experience. Whether you're dancing under the stars or enjoying VIP bottle service, Reina embodies the epitome of Istanbul's high-energy club scene.

**2. Anjelique: Bosphorus Vibes and Cutting-Edge Sounds

Location: Muallim Naci Caddesi Salhane Sokak No:5, Ortaköy

Opening Hours: Varies by event; typically opens in the evening

Overview: Anjelique, nestled on the shores of the Bosphorus, seamlessly combines sophisticated design with cutting-edge sounds. This multi-level venue offers a variety of spaces, including a stylish nightclub, a chic restaurant, and a spacious terrace. Anjelique attracts a diverse crowd seeking an upscale and trendy atmosphere. With its international DJ lineup and immersive ambiance, Anjelique is a premier destination for those looking to dance and revel in the enchanting views of the Bosphorus.

**3. Klein: Intimate Electronic Beats in Beyoğlu

Location: Yeniçarşı Caddesi No:40, Beyoğlu

Opening Hours: Varies by event; typically opens late evening

Overview: Klein, located in the heart of Beyoğlu, is an intimate nightclub dedicated to electronic music. With its minimalist design and cutting-edge sound system, Klein provides an immersive experience for electronic music enthusiasts. The venue hosts both local and international DJs, creating an underground atmosphere that resonates with Istanbul's progressive nightlife scene. Whether you're a dedicated techno fan or an adventurous clubgoer, Klein promises an intimate and electrifying night out.

**4. Sortie: Open-Air Elegance and Diverse Tunes

Location: Muallim Naci Caddesi No:141, Kuruçeşme

Opening Hours: Varies by event; typically opens in the evening

Overview: Sortie, situated in the upscale neighborhood of Kuruçeşme, offers an open-air nightclub experience with a touch of elegance. Surrounded by lush greenery, Sortie features multiple bars, dance floors, and lounges with a diverse range of music. Whether you prefer dancing under the stars or enjoying a cocktail in one of the stylish lounges, Sortie's upscale ambiance and varied music selection cater to a discerning and cosmopolitan crowd.

**5. Suma Beach: Daytime Vibes, Nighttime Revelry

Location: Kilyos, Demirciköy Plajı

Opening Hours: Varies by event; typically opens in the afternoon

Overview: Suma Beach, located on the outskirts of Istanbul in Kilyos, is a unique destination that seamlessly transitions from beach club vibes during the day to a vibrant nightclub atmosphere at night. With its sandy shores, poolside lounges, and an open-air dance floor, Suma Beach offers an immersive experience for those looking to dance under the moonlight. The venue hosts international and local DJs, creating a dynamic environment that captures the spirit of summer nightlife in Istanbul.

**6. Indigo: Trendy Tunes in the Heart of Istanbul

Location: Siraselviler Caddesi No:8, Beyoğlu

Opening Hours: Varies by event; typically opens late evening

Overview: Indigo, nestled in the vibrant district of Beyoğlu, is a trendy nightclub known for its diverse music programming. With a focus on current chart-toppers, as well as electronic and alternative beats, Indigo caters to a young and energetic crowd. The venue's stylish design, vibrant lighting, and energetic atmosphere make it a go-to spot for those seeking a lively night out in the heart of Istanbul.

Live Music Venues

Live Music Venues: Istanbul's Stage for Melodic Nights

Immerse yourself in the soulful melodies and captivating performances of Istanbul's live music scene. From intimate jazz clubs to iconic concert halls, each venue offers a unique setting to experience the diverse sounds that echo through the city.

**1. Babylon Istanbul: Eclectic Beats in Beyoğlu

Location: Şehbender Sk. No:3, Asmalımescit, Beyoğlu

Opening Hours: Varies by event; typically opens in the evening

Overview: Babylon Istanbul, located in the heart of Beyoğlu, is a legendary venue that has been shaping Istanbul's music scene for decades. This intimate yet dynamic space hosts a variety of live performances, from jazz and world music to indie and electronic beats. With its eclectic programming and intimate ambiance, Babylon Istanbul promises unforgettable nights for music enthusiasts. Check their schedule for upcoming concerts and immerse yourself in the rich tapestry of live music.

**2. Nardis Jazz Club: Jazz Rhythms in Galata

Location: Kuledibi Sokak No:14, Galata

Opening Hours: Daily, 8:00 PM - 2:00 AM

Overview: Nardis Jazz Club, nestled in the historic Galata district, is a haven for jazz aficionados. This cozy and welcoming venue features live jazz performances almost every night, showcasing both local talents and international acts. With its intimate setting and commitment to preserving the essence of jazz, Nardis Jazz Club provides an authentic and immersive experience for those seeking the soulful rhythms of this timeless genre.

**3. IF Performance Hall: A Diverse Musical Palette

Location: Kucukbakkalkoy Mahallesi, Kayışdağı Cad. No:1, Ataşehir

Opening Hours: Varies by event; typically opens in the evening

Overview: IF Performance Hall, situated in Ataşehir, stands as a versatile venue that hosts a diverse range of live performances. From rock and pop concerts to classical and world music events, IF Performance Hall caters to a broad spectrum of musical tastes. The state-of-the-art sound system and spacious setting make it a popular choice for both local and international artists. Check their schedule for upcoming shows and immerse yourself in the vibrant world of live music.

**4. Salon İKSV: Cultural Hub for Music and Arts

Location: Nejat Eczacıbaşı Binası Sadi Konuralp Caddesi No:5, Şişhane

Opening Hours: Varies by event; typically opens in the evening

Overview: Salon İKSV, housed in Nejat Eczacıbaşı Building in Şişhane, is a cultural hub that showcases a wide array of artistic performances, including live music concerts. The venue hosts events ranging from indie and alternative bands to classical and experimental music acts. With its commitment to supporting diverse genres and emerging artists, Salon İKSV contributes to Istanbul's vibrant cultural landscape. Explore their schedule to catch a live performance that resonates with your musical preferences.

**5. Harbiye Cemil Topuzlu Open-Air Theater: Symphony Under the Stars

Location: Harbiye Cemil Topuzlu Open-Air Theater, Harbiye, Istanbul

Opening Hours: Varies by event; typically opens in the evening

Overview: Harbiye Cemil Topuzlu Open-Air Theater, located in the picturesque Harbiye area, offers a unique setting for outdoor concerts and live performances. Surrounded by lush greenery, this iconic venue hosts a variety of events, including symphony orchestra concerts, classical music recitals, and contemporary live performances. Whether you're a fan of classical music or eager to discover new sounds, the open-air theater provides a magical atmosphere to enjoy live music under the stars.

**6. KucukCiftlik Park: Concerts in a Green Oasis

Location: KucukCiftlik Park, Harbiye, Istanbul

Opening Hours: Varies by event; typically opens in the evening

Overview: KucukCiftlik Park, situated in the Harbiye neighborhood, serves as a green oasis amidst the bustling city. This outdoor venue hosts a variety of live concerts and events, attracting both local and international artists. From rock and pop to electronic and world music, KucukCiftlik Park offers a spacious and vibrant setting for music enthusiasts. Check their event calendar for upcoming concerts and embrace the joy of live performances in a natural and scenic environment.

Museums and Galleries

Museums and Galleries: Unveiling Istanbul's Cultural Tapestry

Embark on a journey through Istanbul's vibrant cultural scene by exploring its museums and galleries, each offering a unique perspective on the city's rich history and contemporary artistry.

**1. Hagia Sophia Museum: A Timeless Marvel of Architecture

Location: Sultanahmet, Ayasofya Meydanı, Fatih

This is the Opening Hours: Daily, 9:00 AM - 5:00 PM

Cost: Check official website for current admission fees

Overview: Situated in the heart of Sultanahmet, the Hagia Sophia Museum is an architectural marvel that transcends time. Originally a cathedral, then a mosque, and now a museum, it showcases a blend of Byzantine and Ottoman influences. As you walk through its majestic halls, you'll encounter breathtaking mosaics, intricate calligraphy, and a sense of history that spans over a millennium. The Hagia Sophia stands as a testament to Istanbul's rich cultural heritage and is a must-visit for history enthusiasts.

2. Istanbul Modern Art Museum: Contemporary Creations by the Bosphorus

Location: Asmalımescit Mahallesi, Meşrutiyet Cd. No:99, Beyoğlu

Opening Hours: Closed for renovations (check official website for updates)

Cost: Check official website for current admission fees

Overview: The Istanbul Modern Art Museum, located along the Bosphorus, is a hub for contemporary art lovers. While currently closed for renovations, this museum typically features a diverse collection of Turkish and international contemporary art, including paintings, sculptures, and multimedia installations. Its strategic location provides not only a cultural experience but also panoramic views of the Bosphorus, creating a dynamic setting for art appreciation.

**3. Topkapi Palace Museum: Royalty and Intrigue in Every Corner

Location: Sultanahmet, Bab-ı Hümayun Caddesi, Fatih

Opening Hours: Daily, 9:00 AM - 5:00 PM (Closed on Tuesdays)

Cost: Check official website for current admission fees

Istanbul Travel Guide 2024

Overview: Explore the opulent history of the Ottoman Empire at the Topkapi Palace Museum. Nestled in Sultanahmet, this sprawling palace complex was once the residence of Ottoman sultans. Marvel at the intricate design of the Harem, witness the dazzling jewels in the Treasury, and stroll through the lush gardens with stunning views of the Golden Horn. Topkapi Palace Museum invites you to step into the world of royalty and intrigue, offering a glimpse into the grandeur of Istanbul's imperial past.

4. **Pera Museum: Artistic Treasures in Beyoğlu

Location: Asmalımescit Mahallesi, Meşrutiyet Cd. No:65, Beyoğlu

Opening Hours: Check official website for current opening hours

Cost: Check official website for current admission fees

Overview: Pera Museum, situated in the cosmopolitan neighborhood of Beyoğlu, is a haven for art enthusiasts. The museum's eclectic collection includes Orientalist paintings, Anatolian weights and measures, and Turkish ceramics. With its

---

dynamic exhibition programming, Pera Museum introduces visitors to a diverse range of artistic expressions. The elegant surroundings and thought-provoking exhibits make it a cultural oasis in the heart of Istanbul.

**5. Rahmi M. Koç Museum: A Journey Through Industrial History

Location: Hasköy Caddesi No:5, Hasköy, Golden Horn

Opening Hours: Check official website for current opening hours

Cost: Check official website for current admission fees

Overview: Delve into the fascinating world of industrial history at the Rahmi M. Koç Museum, located on the shores of the Golden Horn. This unique museum showcases a vast collection of vehicles, maritime artifacts, and technological innovations. From vintage cars to full-scale replicas of historical ships, each exhibit narrates a captivating story of human ingenuity. The Rahmi M. Koç Museum offers an immersive experience that combines education with the thrill of exploration.

6. Sakıp Sabancı Museum: A Fusion of Art and Nature

Location: Emirgan Sakıp Sabancı Cad. No:42, Emirgan

Opening Hours: Closed for renovations (check official website for updates)

Cost: Check official website for current admission fees

Overview: Nestled in the serene neighborhood of Emirgan, the Sakıp Sabancı Museum seamlessly blends art with nature. Currently closed for renovations, this museum typically hosts an impressive collection of Turkish calligraphy, paintings, and sculptures. The lush gardens surrounding the museum provide a tranquil setting for contemplation, making it a cultural retreat away from the bustle of the city. Explore the intersection of art and nature at the Sakıp Sabancı Museum.

Chapter Eight

Outdoor Activities

Adventure Awaits: Watersports, Hiking, and Trails in Istanbul

Discover the thrill of outdoor activities in

Istanbul, where a perfect blend of watersports, hiking trails, and scenic adventures await. Each experience offers a unique way to explore the natural beauty and recreational opportunities that Istanbul has to offer.

**1. Watersports at Kilyos Beach: Surf, Sail, and Soak in the Sun

Location: Kilyos Beach, Black Sea Coast

Watersports Offered: Windsurfing, Kiteboarding, Jet Skiing

Time to Spend: Half-day to a full day

Price Range: Varies by activity; approximately 150-300 TRY (Turkish Lira)

Kilyos Beach, situated along the Black Sea Coast, is a hotspot for watersports enthusiasts. Dive into the exhilarating world of windsurfing or try your hand at kiteboarding with the gentle Black Sea breeze. For those seeking an adrenaline rush, jet skiing is also available. With rental facilities and instructors on-site, Kilyos Beach provides the perfect setting for a day of sun-soaked watersports adventure.

2. Hiking the Belgrad Forest: Nature's Retreat Within the City

Location: Belgrad Forest, Istanbul

Hiking Trails:* Various trails with different difficulty levels

Time to Spend: Half-day

Price:* Free

Escape the urban hustle and embrace the tranquility of Belgrad Forest, located within the city limits. With numerous hiking trails catering to different skill levels, this lush forest invites you to explore its greenery and serene atmosphere. The Gokturk Trail is a popular choice, offering a moderate hike with scenic views. Pack a picnic, lace up your hiking boots, and immerse yourself in nature without leaving the city.

3. Camlica Hill Trails: Hike with a Panoramic City View

Location: Camlica Hill, Istanbul

Hiking Trails:* Various trails with different difficulty levels

Time to Spend: 2-3 hours

Price:* Free

For a hike with a stunning panoramic view of Istanbul, head to Camlica Hill. With its diverse trails, including the Yavuz Sultan Selim Trail and the Camlica Valley Trail, you can choose an adventure that suits your fitness level. The trails offer a mix of nature and cityscape, making it an ideal escape for those looking for a refreshing hike without venturing far from the heart of Istanbul.

**4. Bosphorus Kayaking Adventure: Paddle Between Continents

Location: Bosphorus Strait, Istanbul

Watersport Offered: Sea Kayaking

Time to Spend: Half-day

Price:* Approximately 150-200 TRY (Turkish Lira)

Experience the unique thrill of kayaking along the Bosphorus Strait, where you can paddle between two continents. This guided sea kayaking adventure allows you to explore Istanbul's iconic landmarks from the water. Marvel at the city's skyline, pass under historic bridges, and discover hidden coves along the way. Suitable for beginners and seasoned kayakers alike, this excursion offers a refreshing perspective of Istanbul's beauty.

**5. Prince Islands Cycling Tour: Explore by Bike

Location: Büyükada, Prince Islands

Cycling Routes:* Various routes exploring the islands

Time to Spend: Full day

Price:* Varies by rental; approximately 50-100 TRY (Turkish Lira)

Escape to the car-free environment of Büyükada in the Prince Islands for a cycling adventure. Rent a bike and explore the island's charming streets, historical architecture, and serene coastline. The island's diverse landscapes, including hills and coastal paths, provide a delightful cycling experience. Take a break at local cafes and enjoy the relaxed pace of island life.

Cultural Experiences

6.1 Turkish Baths (Hamams)

Turkish Baths (Hamams): Immerse Yourself in Tradition and Relaxation

Indulge in a quintessential Turkish experience by visiting a traditional hamam, where centuries-old bathing rituals blend with luxurious relaxation.

These cultural landmarks offer more than just a cleansing ritual; they provide a sensory journey that rejuvenates the body and soul.

Overview:

Description: Hamams have been an integral part of Turkish culture for centuries, serving as communal spaces for socializing, cleansing, and relaxation. Steeped in history and tradition, these bathhouses offer a unique glimpse into the country's rich heritage.

Experience: Upon entering a hamam, you'll be greeted by a serene ambiance characterized by marble interiors, domed ceilings, and soothing music. The experience typically begins with a steam session in the warm, humid environment, followed by a vigorous scrubbing with a kese (exfoliating mitt) to remove dead skin cells and impurities.

Treatment Options: Hamams offer a range of treatments, including traditional soap massages, oil massages, and facials. Skilled attendants, known as tellak (for men) and natır (for women), provide personalized care and attention, ensuring a deeply relaxing and invigorating experience.

Popular Hamams in Istanbul:

1. Çemberlitaş Hamamı: Located near the Grand Bazaar, Çemberlitaş Hamamı is one of Istanbul's oldest and most iconic bathhouses. Dating back to 1584, it features stunning Ottoman architecture and offers a range of traditional treatments.

2. Ayasofya Hürrem Sultan Hamamı: Situated near the Hagia Sophia, this historic hamam was commissioned by Hürrem Sultan, the wife of Suleiman the Magnificent, in the 16th century. With its majestic domes and luxurious treatments, it offers an unforgettable spa experience.

---

3. Kilic Ali Pasa Hamam: Designed by the renowned Ottoman architect Mimar Sinan in the 16th century, Kilic Ali Pasa Hamam is a masterpiece of architectural beauty. Located in the trendy neighborhood of Karaköy, it combines traditional hammam rituals with modern amenities.

Tips for Visiting a Hammam:

- Reservations: It's advisable to make a reservation in advance, especially during peak tourist seasons, to secure your preferred time slot.
- Etiquette: Familiarize yourself with hamam etiquette, such as disrobing in the designated areas and respecting the privacy of other guests.
- Attire: Hamams provide pestemal (traditional Turkish towels) for covering yourself during the bath. Feel free to bring your swimsuit along if you'd like.

- Hydration: Drink plenty of water before and after your hamam experience to stay hydrated and maximize the benefits of the treatment.

Benefits of Visiting a Hammam:

- Relaxation: The warm, steamy environment of a hamam helps relax muscles, alleviate stress, and promote overall well-being.
- Exfoliation: The exfoliating scrubbing process removes dead skin cells, leaving your skin soft, smooth, and radiant.
- Cleansing: Hamam treatments cleanse the body of impurities, toxins, and pollutants, leaving you feeling refreshed and rejuvenated.
- Cultural Immersion: Visiting a hamam offers a unique opportunity to immerse yourself in Turkish culture, traditions, and hospitality,

creating lasting memories of your time in Istanbul.

6.2 Whirling Dervishes Show

Whirling Dervishes Show: A Spiritual and Mesmerizing Experience

Embark on a spiritual journey and witness the mesmerizing Whirling Dervishes Show, a captivating performance that celebrates the ancient tradition of Sufism. This unique cultural experience offers insight into the mystical world of the Whirling Dervishes and their quest for spiritual enlightenment.

Overview:

Description: The Whirling Dervishes Show, also known as the Sema Ceremony, is a traditional ritual performed by members of the Mevlevi Order, a Sufi Muslim sect founded by the poet and mystic Rumi in the 13th century. The ceremony is a form of meditation and prayer, symbolizing the soul's journey towards union with the divine.

Performance: The centerpiece of the show is the mesmerizing whirling dance performed by the dervishes, who spin in graceful, circular motions, symbolizing spiritual ascent and union with God. Accompanied by haunting music and chanting, the performance creates a mesmerizing atmosphere that transports viewers to a transcendent realm.

Symbolism: The whirling dance is rich in symbolism, representing the cosmic dance of the universe, the rotation of the planets, and the journey of the soul towards spiritual enlightenment. Each movement of the dervishes carries deep meaning, reflecting the principles of love, unity, and harmony espoused by Rumi and the Mevlevi Order.

Popular Venues for Whirling Dervishes Shows:

Istanbul Travel Guide 2024

1. Galata Mevlevi Museum: Located in the historic Galata district, the Galata Mevlevi Museum hosts regular Whirling Dervishes performances in a stunning 15th-century tekke (dervish lodge). The intimate setting and spiritual ambiance enhance the experience.

2. Hodjapasha Culture Center: Situated in a beautifully restored hamam near the Hagia Sophia, the Hodjapasha Culture Center offers immersive Whirling Dervishes shows accompanied by live music and mystical lighting effects.

3. Sirkeci Train Station: The iconic Sirkeci Train Station, once the terminus of the Orient Express, hosts special Whirling Dervishes performances in its historic waiting hall. The grandeur of the setting adds to the magical atmosphere of the show.

Tips for Attending a Whirling Dervishes Show:

- Book in Advance: Whirling Dervishes performances are popular among tourists and locals alike, so it's advisable to book your tickets in advance to secure a seat.
- Respectful Attire: Dress modestly out of respect for the spiritual nature of the ceremony. Choose clothing that covers more of your body and leans towards modesty rather than revealing styles.
- Arrive Early: Arrive at the venue early to ensure you have enough time to find parking and settle into your seat before the performance begins.
- Silence and Respect: Maintain silence and refrain from using flash photography or recording devices during the performance to show respect for the sacred nature of the ceremony.

Benefits of Attending a Whirling Dervishes Show:

- Cultural Enrichment: Attending a Whirling Dervishes show offers a profound cultural experience, providing insight into the spiritual traditions and heritage of Turkey.
- Spiritual Reflection: The mesmerizing dance of the dervishes invites contemplation and reflection, offering viewers an opportunity for inner peace and spiritual renewal.
- Artistic Expression: The Whirling Dervishes performance is a beautiful expression of artistry and devotion, showcasing the grace and skill of the dancers and musicians involved.
- Transcendent Experience: The ethereal atmosphere of the Whirling Dervishes show transports viewers to a realm of spiritual

transcendence, leaving a lasting impression of beauty and harmony.

6.3 Traditional Turkish Music and Dance

Traditional Turkish Music and Dance: A Celebration of Culture and Heritage

Delve into the rich tapestry of Turkish culture through the mesmerizing rhythms and vibrant movements of traditional music and dance. From energetic folk dances to soul-stirring melodies, experience the essence of Turkey's cultural heritage in a dynamic and captivating performance.

Overview:

Description: Traditional Turkish music and dance reflect the diverse cultural influences that have shaped the country's history, blending elements of Anatolian, Ottoman, and Arabic traditions. These art forms serve as expressions of joy, love, and community, celebrating life's milestones and seasonal festivities.

Performance: A traditional Turkish music and dance performance typically features a combination of instrumental music, vocal performances, and folk dances. Musicians showcase a variety of instruments, including the oud (lute), ney (flute), and darbuka (drum), while dancers captivate audiences with their skillful footwork and expressive movements.

Variety of Genres: Turkish music encompasses a wide range of genres, from classical Ottoman court music to lively folk tunes and modern interpretations. Similarly, Turkish dance includes a diverse array of styles, such as the energetic folk dances of the Black Sea region, the graceful movements of the Ottoman court dances, and the exuberant performances of the whirling dervishes.

Popular Venues for Traditional Turkish Music and Dance:

1. Istanbul Cultural Centers: Various cultural centers and performance venues throughout Istanbul host regular showcases of traditional Turkish music and dance. These events provide a platform for both established artists and emerging talents to share their art with audiences.

2. Turkish Night Shows: Many restaurants and entertainment venues in Istanbul offer Turkish night shows featuring live music and dance performances. These immersive experiences often include dinner and a cultural program, allowing visitors to enjoy traditional Turkish cuisine while being entertained by talented performers.

3. Folk Music Festivals: Istanbul is home to several folk music festivals that celebrate the rich musical heritage of Turkey. These festivals showcase a diverse lineup of musicians and dancers from

different regions of the country, offering a comprehensive overview of Turkish music and dance traditions.

Benefits of Experiencing Traditional Turkish Music and Dance:

- Cultural Enrichment: Experiencing traditional Turkish music and dance provides a deeper understanding of the country's cultural heritage and artistic traditions.
- Immersion in Local Culture: Attending a traditional music and dance performance allows visitors to immerse themselves in the vibrant rhythms and melodies of Turkish culture, fostering a sense of connection and appreciation for the local community.
- Celebration of Diversity: Turkish music and dance showcase the diverse cultural influences that have shaped the country's

identity, highlighting the richness of Anatolian, Ottoman, and Arabic traditions.

- Entertainment and Enjoyment: Whether watching a lively folk dance performance or listening to soul-stirring melodies, traditional Turkish music and dance offer entertainment and enjoyment for audiences of all ages.

Tips for Enjoying Traditional Turkish Music and Dance:

- Research Performances: Research upcoming performances and events featuring traditional Turkish music and dance in Istanbul, and plan your visit accordingly.
- Respect Cultural Norms: Show respect for cultural norms and etiquette during performances, such as refraining from talking or using electronic devices.

- Engage with Artists: Take the opportunity to engage with artists and performers after the show to learn more about their art and cultural traditions.
- Support Local Artists: Consider purchasing CDs, DVDs, or other merchandise from local artists and performers to support their work and continue the preservation of Turkish music and dance traditions.

6.4 Folklore and Craft Workshops

Folklore and Craft Workshops: Exploring Turkey's Artistic Heritage

Uncover the intricate beauty of Turkey's artistic traditions through immersive folklore and craft workshops. From intricate ceramics to vibrant textile weaving, these hands-on experiences offer a deeper understanding of the country's cultural heritage and provide an opportunity to learn from skilled artisans.

Overview:

Description: Folklore and craft workshops in Turkey offer a glimpse into the country's rich artistic heritage, allowing participants to engage with traditional crafts and techniques passed down through generations. These workshops provide a hands-on experience where visitors can learn about the history, symbolism, and significance of various art forms while creating their own unique works of art.

Activities: Depending on the workshop, participants may have the opportunity to learn a variety of traditional crafts, including pottery, calligraphy, marbling (ebru), carpet weaving, and embroidery. Guided by experienced artisans, participants can explore different techniques and create their own masterpieces to take home as souvenirs.

Cultural Immersion: Folklore and craft workshops offer more than just a creative outlet; they provide a deeper connection to Turkish culture and heritage. Participants gain insight into the stories, symbolism, and cultural significance behind each craft, fostering a greater appreciation for the country's artistic traditions.

Popular Folklore and Craft Workshops:

1. Pottery Workshops: Explore the art of pottery making at workshops located in pottery-producing regions like Çanakkale, Avanos, and Çini. Learn to shape clay on a pottery wheel, decorate ceramics with traditional motifs, and gain an appreciation for the craftsmanship involved in this ancient art form.

2. Turkish Carpet Weaving Workshops: Discover the intricate art of Turkish carpet weaving at workshops in carpet-producing regions such as Cappadocia, Konya, and Kayseri. Watch skilled weavers at work, learn about different weaving techniques and patterns, and even try your hand at knotting a small carpet.

3. Calligraphy and Marbling Workshops: Immerse yourself in the elegant art of calligraphy and marbling (ebru) at workshops in Istanbul and other major cities. Learn the basics of Arabic script, practice different calligraphy styles, and create your own marbled paper using colorful dyes and swirling patterns.

Benefits of Participating in Folklore and Craft Workshops:

- Hands-On Learning: Folklore and craft workshops offer a hands-on learning experience, allowing participants to engage with traditional crafts and techniques under the guidance of skilled artisans.

- Cultural Enrichment: By learning about the history, symbolism, and significance of various art forms, participants gain a deeper understanding of Turkish culture and heritage.

- Creative Expression: Participants have the opportunity to unleash their creativity and express themselves through their own unique works of art, whether it's a handcrafted pottery piece, a woven carpet, or a calligraphic masterpiece.
- Souvenir Creation: Workshop participants can take home their creations as souvenirs, providing tangible mementos of their time spent in Turkey and serving as reminders of the rich artistic traditions they've experienced.

Tips for Participating in Folklore and Craft Workshops:
- Plan in Advance: Research workshop options and book your spot in advance, especially during peak tourist seasons when workshops may fill up quickly.

- Dress Comfortably: Wear comfortable clothing and shoes that you don't mind getting dirty, especially for hands-on workshops like pottery making or marbling.
- Be Open-Minded: Approach the workshop with an open mind and a willingness to learn. Embrace the opportunity to try something new and step outside your comfort zone.
- Ask Questions: Take advantage of the opportunity to ask the workshop instructors questions and learn more about the techniques, traditions, and cultural significance of the craft.

Events and Festivals

Immerse yourself in Istanbul's vibrant events and festivals.

Participate in Istanbul's yearly events and festivals to immerse yourself in the city's vibrant cultural tapestry. From ancient festivals to modern gatherings, each event lends a new dimension to the city's lively environment. Here's a look at the yearly event schedule, which offers amazing experiences throughout the year.

**1. Istanbul Film Festival: A Cinematic Extravaganza.

The Istanbul Film Festival, held annually in March–April, honors cinema with a broad selection of local and foreign films. This festival, organized by the Istanbul Foundation for Culture and Arts, brings together cinema aficionados, directors, and actors from all over the globe. With screenings, premieres, and fascinating talks, the festival provides a stimulating environment for cinephiles to discover the best in cinematic storytelling.

**2. Tulip Festival: Blooms over the City

Date: April

Overview: In April, Istanbul transforms into a riot of hues as millions of tulips blossom over parks, gardens, and public areas. The Istanbul Tulip Festival celebrates spring's advent with beautiful displays of tulips in a variety of colors. From Emirgan Park to Gulhane Park, the city transforms into a beautiful wonderland. Visit the wonderfully manicured regions and engage in cultural activities for a gorgeous and culturally stimulating experience.

**3. International Istanbul Music Festival: Harmony Across Genres (June–July) The Istanbul Foundation for Culture and Arts hosts the International Istanbul Music Festival in June and July, which attracts world-class performers and orchestras. The festival's schedule is wide, including classical, jazz, and world music acts. Venues like the Hagia Irene and Harbiye Cemil Topuzlu Open-Air Theater become venues for melodic brilliance, providing a peaceful environment for music lovers.

**4. Istanbul Jazz Festival: Rhythms Under the Stars.

Date: June–July

Overview: Every June and July, jazz fans go to Istanbul for the annual Istanbul Jazz Festival. This festival converts renowned sites such as the Harbiye Cemil Topuzlu Open-Air Theater and different jazz clubs into platforms where legendary performances take place. From classic jazz to experimental sounds, the festival's schedule is broad, bringing together local and international musicians to create an appealing musical environment beneath the city's night sky.

**5. Istanbul Biennial: Contemporary Art Extravaganza.

Date: Every two years on odd-numbered years.

Overview: The Istanbul Biennial, held every two years in odd-numbered years, is a worldwide festival of contemporary art. The Istanbul Foundation for Culture and Arts organizes this event, which converts diverse venues, galleries, and historical buildings into immersive art environments. The biennial features the work of both new and renowned artists, challenging the frontiers of creative expression and provoking discussions about social challenges.

6. Republic Day celebrations: commemorating Turkish independence.

On October 29, Turkey celebrates Republic Day, which commemorates the creation of the Republic of Turkey in 1923. Istanbul comes alive with patriotic festivals, including parades, concerts, and fireworks. Taksim Square and the Bosphorus, two of the city's most famous sights, became popular gathering places. Join the people in celebrating the spirit of togetherness and pride on this important national holiday.

**7. Istanbul International Architecture and Urban Films Festival: Explore Cityscapes Through Film

Date: November.

Overview: Held in November, the Istanbul International Architecture and Urban Films Festival allows filmmakers and aficionados to investigate the link between architecture, urban planning, and cinema. The festival explores how cinema portrays and interprets the built environment via screenings, conversations, and installations. This one-of-a-kind event encourages discussion regarding the relationship between cinematic narrative and the urban landscape.

**8. New Year's Eve on the Bosphorus: Celebrating the New Year in Style

Date: December 31.

Overview: When the clock strikes midnight on New Year's Eve, Istanbul turns into a stunning display of lights and festivities. Cruise around the Bosphorus to see spectacular fireworks illuminate the city skyline. Many restaurants, clubs, and venues conduct special events, creating a stylish and joyful environment to celebrate the new year.

Plan your vacation around these exciting events and festivals to fully immerse yourself in Istanbul's cultural diversity. Whether you're a film aficionado, music lover, or art enthusiast, Istanbul's yearly calendar offers a colorful and varied experience all year.

Notable Festivals

Notable Festivals in Istanbul: Highlights for 2024
Explore Istanbul's cultural diversity in 2024 with a list of important events that promise to capture your senses and immerse you in the city's dynamic environment. From traditional festivities to modern presentations, these festivals provide unique experiences for both tourists and residents.

**1. Istanbul Tulip Festival, April

Overview: Witness Istanbul in full bloom at the annual Istanbul Tulip Festival, which celebrates the entrance of spring. Throughout April, the city changes into a tapestry of colorful tulip displays in parks, gardens, and public areas. Experience vibrant colors, cultural activities, and the city's stunning tulip blooms.

2. International Istanbul Music Festival, June–July.
Overview: Enhance your musical experience at the

International Istanbul Music Festival, a prominent event featuring renowned performers and orchestras. This festival, held in June and July, features a variety of genres, such as classical, jazz, and world music. The city's iconic venues, such as the Hagia Irene and Harbiye Cemil Topuzlu Open-Air Theater, provide mesmerizing performances beneath the city's lovely sky.

3. Istanbul Jazz Festival

Date: June–July

Overview: Experience a soulful journey through the sounds of jazz at the Istanbul Jazz Festival, held in June and July. This famous event turns the city into a jazz hotspot, with performances by both local and international performers. Istanbul's diverse venues, from open-air theaters to intimate jazz clubs, provide the ideal backdrop for an unforgettable musical experience.

** 4. Istanbul Biennial

Date: September–November

Overview: Immerse yourself in the world of contemporary art at the Istanbul Biennial, held every two years in odd-numbered years. In 2024, this worldwide event will highlight the work of cutting-edge artists, breaking conventional limits and dealing with critical social challenges. Various locations across the city transform into temporary art spaces, encouraging guests to discover novel forms of creation.

**5. Republic Day Celebrations

Date: October 29

Overview: Join locals to celebrate Turkey's Republic Day on October 29. This national holiday commemorates the creation of the Republic of Turkey in 1923 and is celebrated with patriotic parades, concerts, and lively celebrations.

Experience the sense of solidarity and pride as Istanbul comes alive with patriotic zeal, producing a lasting impression across the city.

6. Istanbul International Architecture and Urban Films Festival

Date: November

Overview: Explore the relationship between architecture, urban planning, and film at the Istanbul International Architecture and Urban Films Festival. This one-of-a-kind festival, held every November, investigates how films depict the built environment. Participants participate in a thought-provoking discourse about the dynamic link between architecture and film via screenings, talks, and installations.

**7. New Year's Eve along the Bosphorus

Date: December 31

Overview: Enjoy a magnificent New Year's Eve party along the Bosphorus in Istanbul. Cruise the renowned Strait and experience a spectacular display of fireworks that illuminates the city skyline. Join the celebrations at numerous locations, including restaurants, clubs, and outdoor areas, as Istanbul celebrates the new year with style and enthusiasm.

Chapter Nine

Day Trips from Istanbul

Day Trips from Istanbul: Exploring Beyond the City

While Istanbul offers a wealth of attractions and experiences, venturing beyond its bustling streets unveils a treasure trove of historical sites, natural wonders, and charming towns waiting to be discovered. Embark on a series of unforgettable day trips from Istanbul, each offering a unique glimpse into Turkey's diverse landscapes and cultural heritage.

From the ancient ruins of Ephesus to the serene landscapes of the Princes' Islands, these day trips promise adventure, relaxation, and a deeper appreciation for the beauty and history of this fascinating country. Join us as we journey beyond the city limits and explore the wonders that await just a short distance from Istanbul.

10.1 Princes' Islands

Princes' Islands: Tranquility Near the Bustle

Escape the hustle and bustle of Istanbul and embark on a serene journey to the Princes' Islands, a picturesque archipelago in the Sea of Marmara. Comprising nine islands, with Büyükada being the largest and most visited, these car-free havens offer a peaceful retreat from the city's frenetic pace.

Overview:

Description: The Princes' Islands, known as Adalar in Turkish, have long been favored as summer retreats by Istanbul's elite. With their charming wooden mansions, lush pine forests, and crystal-clear waters, these islands exude an old-world charm that transports visitors back in time.

Activities: Explore Büyükada's quaint streets by foot, bicycle, or horse-drawn carriage (fayton), admiring the island's elegant Ottoman-era architecture and panoramic views of the sea. Indulge in fresh seafood at waterfront restaurants, swim in secluded coves, or simply relax on the sandy beaches.

Historical Significance: The Princes' Islands have a rich history dating back to Byzantine and Ottoman times. During the Byzantine period, exiled emperors and princes were banished to the islands, giving rise to their name. Later, in the 19th century, the islands became popular among Istanbul's aristocracy, who built summer mansions and villas amid the island's natural beauty.

How to Get There:

Ferry: Regular ferries depart from Istanbul's Kabataş and Eminönü ferry terminals to Büyükada and the other Princes' Islands. The ferry journey takes approximately one to two hours, depending on the departure point and sea conditions.

Tips: Purchase your ferry tickets in advance, especially during the summer months when the islands are popular destinations for both locals and tourists. Arrive early to secure a seat on the ferry and enjoy the scenic journey across the Sea of Marmara.

Highlights of Büyükada:

1. Aya Yorgi Church and Monastery: Perched atop Büyükada's highest hill, Aya Yorgi offers panoramic

views of the island and the surrounding sea. Visitors can climb the hill or take a horse-drawn carriage to reach the church and monastery, which are dedicated to St. George.

2. Hagia Triada Monastery: Explore the historic Hagia Triada Monastery, a Greek Orthodox monastery dating back to the 19th century. Admire its beautiful architecture and serene atmosphere, and learn about its significance in the island's history.

3. Buyukada Pier: Take a leisurely stroll along the Büyükada Pier, lined with charming cafes, restaurants, and souvenir shops. Enjoy views of the island's colorful waterfront and watch as horse-drawn carriages transport visitors along the promenade.

10.2 Troy and Gallipoli

Troy and Gallipoli: Journeys Through History

Embark on a journey through time to two iconic destinations steeped in history and legend: Troy and Gallipoli. These sites, each with its own significance and tales of heroism, offer profound insights into Turkey's ancient past and its pivotal role in shaping the course of history.

Overview:

Description: Troy, the legendary city immortalized in Homer's epic poem, the "Iliad," and Gallipoli, the site of a pivotal World War I battle, stand as

---

enduring symbols of courage, sacrifice, and resilience. Visiting these historic sites provides a poignant reminder of the human experience across the ages.

Troy: Located in the northwestern province of Çanakkale, Troy is an archaeological site that dates back over 4,000 years. It is famously known as the setting of the Trojan War, as described in Homer's epic poems. Explore the ancient ruins, including the imposing walls of Troy's citadel, and unravel the mysteries of this legendary city.

Gallipoli: Situated on the Gallipoli Peninsula in the Çanakkale Province, Gallipoli is renowned for the Gallipoli Campaign of World War I. The site witnessed one of the most significant battles of the war, where Allied forces, including troops from Australia and New Zealand (ANZAC), fought against Ottoman forces. Pay tribute to the thousands of soldiers who lost their lives in this historic conflict at the poignant memorials and cemeteries that dot the landscape.

How to Get There:

Troy: Troy is accessible by road from Istanbul, with a journey time of approximately five to six hours. Alternatively, guided tours from Istanbul to Troy are available, providing transportation and informative commentary along the way.

Gallipoli: Gallipoli is also reachable by road from Istanbul, with a travel time of around four to five hours. Guided tours offer convenient transportation and expert guidance to explore the battlefields, memorials, and cemeteries of Gallipoli.

Highlights of Troy and Gallipoli:

Troy:

- The Trojan Horse: Marvel at the iconic wooden replica of the Trojan Horse, a symbol of cunning and deception in the legendary siege of Troy.
- Ruins of Troy: Explore the archaeological site of Troy, including the remains of ancient city walls, residential buildings, and temples, which provide insight into daily life in antiquity.

Gallipoli:

- ANZAC Cove: Stand on the shores of ANZAC Cove, where Australian and New Zealand troops landed on April 25, 1915, marking the beginning of the Gallipoli Campaign.
- Lone Pine Cemetery: Pay homage to the fallen soldiers at Lone Pine Cemetery, one of the largest Commonwealth cemeteries in Gallipoli, where thousands of Allied soldiers are laid to rest.

10.3 Ephesus

Ephesus: Journey Through Ancient Glory

Step back in time and immerse yourself in the grandeur of Ephesus, one of the most well-preserved ancient cities in the Mediterranean. From its majestic monuments to its bustling streets,

Ephesus offers a glimpse into the rich tapestry of ancient life and civilization.

Overview:

Description: Ephesus, located near the modern-day town of Selçuk in the Izmir Province, was once a thriving Greek and Roman city and a bustling hub of commerce, culture, and spirituality. Today, its impressive ruins stand as a testament to its former glory, drawing visitors from around the world to marvel at its architectural wonders and historical significance.

Historical Significance: Founded in the 10th century BC, Ephesus flourished as a major center of trade and culture under Greek and Roman rule. It was famed for its Temple of Artemis, one of the Seven Wonders of the Ancient World, as well as its magnificent Library of Celsus and Theater of Ephesus, which could seat over 25,000 spectators.

Archaeological Site: Explore the extensive archaeological site of Ephesus, which encompasses well-preserved ruins dating from various periods of its history. Highlights include the monumental Library of Celsus, the grand Theater of Ephesus, the Terrace Houses with their intricate mosaics and frescoes, and the Temple of Hadrian adorned with elegant reliefs.

How to Get There:

Ephesus is easily accessible from major cities such as Izmir and Kusadasi by road. Guided tours and public transportation options, including buses and taxis, are available for visitors wishing to explore the site.

Highlights of Ephesus:

- Library of Celsus: Admire the facade of the Library of Celsus, an iconic symbol of Ephesus known for its striking architectural design and richly decorated interior. Learn about the history of the library and its role as a center of learning and scholarship in antiquity.

- Theater of Ephesus: Marvel at the grandeur of the Theater of Ephesus, one of the largest ancient theaters in the world. Imagine the performances and events that once took place within its walls as you take in the panoramic views of the surrounding landscape.
- House of the Virgin Mary: Visit the nearby House of the Virgin Mary, a sacred site believed to be the final resting place of Mary, the mother of Jesus. Discover the spiritual significance of this pilgrimage site and experience a moment of reflection and reverence.

10.4 Bursa

Bursa: Gateway to Ottoman Heritage

Discover the rich tapestry of Ottoman history and culture in the enchanting city of Bursa, nestled at the foot of Mount Uludağ. As the first capital of the Ottoman Empire, Bursa boasts a wealth of architectural treasures, lush greenery, and vibrant bazaars, inviting visitors to explore its centuries-old legacy.

Overview:

Description: Bursa, located in northwestern Turkey, is renowned for its historical significance, natural beauty, and cultural heritage. Once a thriving center of trade and commerce along the Silk Road, Bursa flourished under Ottoman rule, leaving behind a legacy of stunning mosques, elegant tombs, and atmospheric bazaars.

Historical Significance: Founded by the ancient Greeks as Prusa, Bursa later became the capital of the Ottoman Empire in the 14th century, serving as a political, economic, and cultural hub for centuries. Its strategic location between Europe and Asia made it a vital link in the Silk Road trade route, contributing to its prosperity and cultural diversity.

Architectural Gems: Explore Bursa's architectural wonders, including the UNESCO-listed Bursa Historic Area, which encompasses iconic landmarks such as the Grand Mosque (Ulu Cami), the Green

Mosque (Yeşil Cami), and The tomb of Osman Gazi, who established the Ottoman Empire.

How to Get There:

Bursa is easily accessible from Istanbul by ferry or bus, with frequent services departing from various points in the city. The ferry journey across the Sea of Marmara offers scenic views of Istanbul's skyline and the surrounding coastline, while buses provide a convenient and comfortable option for overland travel.

Highlights of Bursa:

- Grand Mosque (Ulu Cami): Admire the magnificent architecture of the Grand Mosque, with its imposing domes, intricate calligraphy, and stunning interior decorations. Marvel at the mosque's 20 domes, 12 pillars, and impressive courtyard, which reflect the grandeur of Ottoman design.

Istanbul Travel Guide 2024

- Green Mosque (Yeşil Cami): Explore the Green Mosque, a masterpiece of Islamic architecture known for its exquisite turquoise tiles, intricate woodwork, and serene courtyard. Admire the harmony of geometric patterns and floral motifs that adorn the mosque's interior, creating a tranquil ambiance for prayer and reflection.
- Bazaars and Markets: Wander through Bursa's bustling bazaars and markets, where the sights, sounds, and aromas of Turkish culture come alive. Explore the historic Silk Market (Koza Han), sample local delicacies at the Covered Bazaar (Bedesten), and shop for traditional crafts, textiles, and souvenirs in the Old Town.

Chapter Ten

Practical Information

Language and Communication

Prepare for a seamless experience in Istanbul by familiarizing yourself with essential practical information. From language considerations to communication tips, this guide will help you navigate the vibrant city with confidence.

1. Official Language: Turkish

Overview: The official language in Istanbul is Turkish. While English is widely spoken in tourist areas, learning a few basic Turkish phrases can enhance your interactions and showcase your appreciation for the local culture. Here are a few useful phrases:

- Merhaba (mehr-HAH-bah): Hello
- Teşekkür ederim (teh-shehk-KOOR ed-EH-rim): Thank you
- Evet (EH-vet): Yes
- Hayır (HAH-yuhr): No
- Lütfen (LOOT-fen): Please
- Günaydın (goo-NAH-ydun): Good morning
- Esenlikler dilerim (ES-en-lik-lair dee-lair-IM): Goodbye

2. English in tourist areas.

In prominent tourist sites, English is commonly spoken, and signage and menus are often accessible in English. However, walking into local markets and neighborhoods may require a greater dependence on basic Turkish or a translation tool.

**3. Translation App Recommendations: Consider installing translation tools like Google Translate or Microsoft Translator for on-the-go help. These applications may help you navigate menus, connect with locals, and read street signs.

**4. Currency: Turkish Lira (TRY) Overview: The Turkish Lira (TRY) is the official currency of Istanbul. Credit cards are generally accepted, particularly in tourist locations, although it's best to have some local cash for smaller places or markets.

**5. Tipping Etiquette Guidelines: Tipping is traditional in Istanbul. In restaurants, it is customary to leave a tip of 5–10% of the entire cost. Tipping is also appreciated for services such as taxi rides, hotel workers, and tour guides.

**6. Emergency numbers

Essential Numbers: In the event of an emergency, call the following numbers:

Medical Emergency: 112

Police: 155.

Fire Department: 110.

**7. Public Transportation Overview: Istanbul has a comprehensive public transportation system, including buses, trams, metros, and ferries.

Istanbulkart, a rechargeable smart card, is a handy method of paying for public transit. It works on buses, trams, and ferries.

**8. Time Zone Information: Istanbul uses Turkey Time (TRT), which is UTC+3. Please calibrate your watch or gadgets upon arrival. **9. Wi-Fi Availability

Tip: Many cafés, restaurants, and public locations in Istanbul have free Wi-Fi. In addition, prominent hotels and motels provide Wi-Fi to their visitors.

**10. Local Etiquette Guidelines: Use local etiquette to greet individuals with a smile and courteous comments. When visiting mosques or religious institutions, dress modestly and take off your shoes. It is traditional to greet shop and restaurant personnel while arriving and leaving.

Incorporating these practical recommendations into your trip plans will help you navigate Istanbul more easily. Whether you're speaking with locals, experiencing the city's public transit, or immersing yourself in local culture, these tips can help you have a memorable and pleasurable time in Istanbul.

Safety Tips

While Istanbul is typically a safe location for tourists, it is important to be educated and follow best practices to ensure a safe and happy visit. Here are some safety guidelines to help you travel to Istanbul confidently:

**1. Stay informed: Be aware of the current situation in Istanbul and any travel warnings issued by your own country. Follow local news sources and check for official updates.

**2. Select reputable accommodations.

Recommendation: Choose well-established and reliable hotels. Read reviews, compare ratings, and choose lodgings in safe neighborhoods.

Sultanahmet and Taksim are popular tourist destinations.

3. Protect your belongings.

Guidelines: Be cautious with your possessions, particularly in busy locations and on public transit. Use anti-theft bags, safeguard valuables, and be aware of your surroundings.

**4. Be aware of scams.

Caution: Be wary of popular travel scams such as overpriced merchandise, unlicensed advice, and counterfeit tickets. Only employ approved tour providers, and be wary of unwanted help.

**5. Choose Reliable Transit Tip: Consider official taxis, ride-sharing services, or public transit. Take caution while taking rides from strangers.

6. Respect local customs and traditions, particularly at religious places. When visiting mosques, dress modestly and follow any recommendations specified by the website.

**7. Stay Hydrated and Sun-Protected

Recommendations: Istanbul enjoys mild temperatures, particularly during the summer. Stay hydrated, use sunscreen, and seek shade to minimize heat-related problems.

**8. Emergency Contacts Essential numbers: Familiarize yourself with emergency contact numbers, such as medical (112), police (155), and fire (110). Make these statistics readily accessible.

**9. Stay in well-lit areas at night as a precaution. When visiting the city at night, stay in well-lit and crowded areas. To improve your safety, avoid streets that are poorly lit or vacant.

**10. COVID-19 Precautions.

Current Consideration: Stay up to speed on the newest COVID-19 recommendations and safeguards. Follow health standards, use masks in crowded situations, and abide by any local rules.

11. Trust your instincts.

Guidance: Trust your intuition. Remove yourself from a situation that makes you feel uncomfortable or dangerous. Be aware of your surroundings and use care in unusual situations.

**12. Learn basic local words Tip: Knowing a few basic Turkish words will assist with communication and managing local situations. Locals appreciate the effort, which might improve your experience.

**13. Travel Insurance Prepare: Get adequate travel insurance that covers medical emergencies, trip cancellations, and other unexpected occurrences.

14. Local currency and ATMs Tip: Use well-lit, secure ATMs to withdraw local currency. Inform your bank about your trip dates to prevent any card complications.

Health and Medical Services.

Health and Medical Services: Staying Healthy in Istanbul

When visiting Istanbul, it's important to prioritize

your health and well-being. Familiarize yourself with the various health and medical services so that you can handle any unanticipated emergencies with ease.

**1. Health Precautions Guidance: Prioritize your health by following common travel health precautions. Maintain hydration, maintain proper hand hygiene, and use caution while consuming food and liquids.

**2. Medical Facilities Overview: Istanbul has contemporary medical facilities and hospitals with excellent technologies. For medical emergencies, contact recognized facilities such as Acıbadem Hospital, Memorial Hospital, or American Hospital Istanbul.

**3. Pharmacies Information: Pharmacies (eczane) are easily accessible in Istanbul. Look for the green neon cross sign; most pharmacists know English. Common drugs may need a prescription, so speak with a local pharmacy or visit a clinic for advice.

**4. Emergency Medical Services.

Essential Numbers: In the event of a medical emergency, call 112 to contact emergency medical assistance. This line is open 24 hours a day, seven days a week, and operators speak English.

**5. Travel Insurance Recommendation: Obtain adequate travel insurance that covers medical emergencies. Check the coverage for hospitalization, medical repatriation, and any other health issues you may have.

**6. COVID-19 Considerations.

Current guidelines: Keep up with the newest COVID-19 rules and practices. Follow local restrictions, use masks in busy situations, and take health and safety precautions.

**7. Vaccine Advice: Before flying to Istanbul, check with your healthcare professional about required immunizations. Routine immunizations, as well as vaccines specific to your trip plan, may be suggested.

**8. English-speaking physicians In Istanbul, many physicians and healthcare workers speak English, particularly at large hospitals and clinics. When seeking medical treatment, it is essential that you ask about English-speaking professionals.

**9. Water Safety Guidelines: While tap water in Istanbul is typically safe for brushing teeth, it is best to consume bottled or filtered water. Be wary of ice in beverages and undercooked meals from street sellers.

**10. Precautions for Specific Conditions.

Consideration: If you have any special health issues or concerns, check with your doctor before flying. Bring any required medicines, prescriptions, and a basic first-aid kit.

**11. Medical Tourism Services Information: Istanbul is a popular destination for medical tourism, providing a variety of healthcare services including cosmetic surgery, dental operations, and wellness treatments. Make sure you select

---

authorized and respected facilities.

**12: Local Health Hotlines

Essential Numbers: Familiarize oneself with local health hotlines.

Ambulance (Medical Emergency): 112.

Poison Control: 114.

**13. Mosquito Protection Advice: If you want to explore regions with a greater risk of mosquito-borne illnesses, consider applying mosquito repellent and wearing long sleeves and trousers.

**14. Pharmacies having extended hours.

Tip: Some pharmacies in high-traffic locations and tourist destinations may have extended hours, providing services beyond normal business hours. Look for signage suggesting 24-hour pharmacies.

Prioritize your well-being by remaining aware of accessible health services, implementing preventative actions, and having access to necessary information. With these tips, you may easily negotiate health-related issues throughout your stay in Istanbul.

Useful apps and resources.

Useful Apps and Resources for Easy Travel in Istanbul

Make the most of your Istanbul trip by adding these crucial applications and tools to your travel toolbox. These programs, which include navigation, language translation, and currency conversion, will improve your experience in this dynamic city.

14.1 Navigation Apps: Google Maps: This essential tool offers precise maps, real-time traffic updates, and instructions for walking, cycling, or driving. Explore Istanbul's streets, identify landmarks, and plan efficient routes.

Moovit provides real-time arrival information for Istanbul's public transit system, including buses, trams, metros, and ferries. This comprehensive transportation software allows you to smoothly plan your travels.

Use Uber or BiTaksi for dependable and convenient transportation. Easily hail a vehicle and get to your location with ease.

14.2 Language Translation Apps: Google Translate: Description: Use Google Translate to break down language boundaries. Translate text, audio, and graphics. Download language packs for offline usage, making it a useful tool for communicating in a variety of settings.

Description: Microsoft Translator provides real-time language translation for text and voice. Use it for chats, signs, or menus, and use the offline mode to translate without an online connection.

iTranslate is a user-friendly translation tool that supports several languages. It has capabilities like speech recognition and the ability to store frequently used words for future reference.

14.3 Currency Converters: XE Currency: Description: Keep track of currency exchange rates with XE Currency. This program offers real-time rates, historical data, and the ability to monitor several currencies, allowing you to make more educated financial choices.

Currency Converter Plus:

Currency Converter Plus uses an easy UI to make currency conversions easier. It has offline capability, making it ideal for rapid conversions that do not need an internet connection.

Description: Easy Currency Converter is a simple program for rapid currency conversion. Its simple design and rapid results make it an excellent tool for keeping track of your costs throughout your journey to Istanbul.

15 Useful Websites for Planning Your Istanbul Adventure

Discover the richness of Istanbul with these helpful websites that offer valuable information, insights, and tools to enhance your travel experience. From planning your itinerary to exploring local culture, these websites cover various aspects of your Istanbul adventure.

1. www.goturkey.com:

Description: Turkey's official tourism website provides comprehensive information about Istanbul's attractions, events, and practical travel tips. Explore cultural highlights, plan itineraries, and stay updated on the latest travel news.

2. www.howtoistanbul.com:

Description: HowToIstanbul is a valuable resource for travelers, offering guides on attractions, neighborhoods, and practical tips for navigating the city. Discover hidden gems and cultural insights to make the most of your visit.

3. www.istanbul.com:

Description: Istanbul.com is a one-stop platform for all things Istanbul. From event listings and restaurant recommendations to travel guides and local news, this website covers a wide range of topics to assist your journey.

4. www.timeout.com/istanbul:

Description: Time Out Istanbul is your go-to guide for events, dining, and entertainment in the city. Stay updated on the latest happenings, explore local culture, and find recommendations for dining and nightlife.

5. www.enjoy-istanbul.com:

Description: Enjoy Istanbul offers insightful articles, travel guides, and tips to help you navigate the city. From historical sites to contemporary attractions, this website provides a well-rounded view of Istanbul's offerings.

6. www.istanbulinsider.com:

Description: Istanbul Insider caters to both tourists and expats, offering practical advice on living and exploring Istanbul. Find tips on local markets, transportation, and cultural experiences to make your stay more enjoyable.

7. www.allaboutturkey.com/istanbul:

Description: All About Turkey's Istanbul section provides in-depth information about the city's history, landmarks, and neighborhoods. Explore cultural aspects, historical insights, and travel tips on this informative site.

8. www.yabangee.com:

Description: Yabangee is a community-focused platform offering insights into Istanbul's expat scene. Discover events, cultural happenings, and practical advice for newcomers to Istanbul.

9. www.weather.com:

Description: Stay ahead of the weather with The Weather Channel. Check current conditions, forecasts, and plan your daily activities in Istanbul with real-time weather updates.

10. www.istanbulfind.com:

Description: Istanbul Find is a travel and lifestyle platform offering curated guides, local recommendations, and event listings. Dive into the city's diverse offerings and find hidden gems with their insightful content.

11. www.metro.istanbul:

Description: Istanbul Metropolitan Municipality's official website for public transportation. Access information on metro, tram, bus services, and use the journey planner to navigate the city seamlessly.

Istanbul Travel Guide 2024

12. www.turkishairlines.com**:**

Description: Turkish Airlines' official website is a convenient platform for booking flights, managing reservations, and staying informed about the airline's services. Plan your journey to Istanbul with ease.

13. www.istanbul.com/en**:**

Description: Istanbul.com's English version provides a user-friendly interface with valuable information on attractions, dining, and events. Explore the city's offerings and plan your itinerary with this comprehensive resource.

14. www.turkeytravelplanner.com**:**

Description: Turkey Travel Planner offers practical travel advice, itineraries, and tips for exploring Istanbul and other destinations in Turkey. Plan your trip efficiently with the insights provided on this website.

---

15. www.navigaia.com:

Description: Navigaia offers interactive maps and guides for various cities, including Istanbul. Access detailed maps, points of interest, and helpful information to navigate the city with ease.

These websites cover a spectrum of topics, from travel planning and cultural insights to practical tips for navigating Istanbul. Use them to streamline your journey and make the most of your time in this captivating city.

Conclusion

As we wrap up our complete guide to Istanbul in 2024, we urge you to go on a trip filled with cultural magnificence, historical wonders, and the dynamic energy that distinguishes this captivating city. Istanbul, where East meets West, entices visitors with its ageless appeal, combining the old and contemporary in a harmonic dance.

Istanbul Travel Guide 2024

In 2024, Istanbul will be a tapestry of experiences, beckoning you to explore its different districts, sample its delicious food, and immerse yourself in the legends carved within its historic walls. From the ancient areas of Sultanahmet to the vibrant energy of Taksim, every turn exposes a new aspect of Istanbul's attraction.

The city's historic sites, such as the Hagia Sophia and Blue Mosque, blend with the vibrant districts of Karaköy and Kadıköy. As you walk through the picturesque streets, you'll see the intersection of history and innovation, resulting in a vibrant and ever-changing tapestry.

Our curated tour will transport you through time and culture, providing insights on getting there, navigating the city, and enjoying the greatest of Istanbul's attractions. Whether you're attracted to the grandeur of Topkapi Palace, the bustling shops of the Grand and Spice Bazaars, or the tranquil beauty of the Bosphorus, Istanbul has something to offer everyone.

Dive into Istanbul's gastronomic treasures, from delicious kebabs to scrumptious desserts, and let your taste buds dance to the symphony of flavors that defines Turkish cuisine. Explore the city's numerous neighborhoods, each with its own distinct charm and character, presenting a rich tapestry of experiences for every visitor.

As you plan your stay, keep practical information, safety guidelines, and health services in mind to ensure smooth and safe travel. Use the suggested applications, websites, and tools to travel Istanbul with ease and make the most of your stay in this fascinating city.

In 2024, Istanbul beckons not just as a destination but also as a riveting story waiting to be revealed. Whether you're a history buff, a gastronomic traveler, or looking for exciting adventures, Istanbul will leave an everlasting impact on your travel memories.

Istanbul Travel Guide 2024

So, while you walk the cobblestone streets and inhale the aromas of spice-filled marketplaces, let Istanbul weave its charm around you. May your voyage be full of exploration, amazement, and Turkish hospitality. Istanbul awaits, eager to disclose its riches and leave you with memories that will last a lifetime.

7-day itinerary.

7-day Istanbul itinerary: A Journey through Time and Culture

Day one: Exploring Sultanahmet

Morning: Begin your adventure in the heart of Istanbul, visiting Sultanahmet. Explore the magnificent Hagia Sophia, a masterpiece of Byzantine architecture, with its complex domes and exquisite mosaics.

Afternoon: Learn about the Blue Mosque's history and its beautiful blue tiles. Stroll around the historic Hippodrome Square and discover its historical importance.

Evening: End the day with a visit to Topkapi Palace, the historic home of Ottoman sultans. Wander around the royal grounds and see the spectacular views of the Bosphorus.

Day Two: Bosphorus Exploration

Morning: Take a Bosphorus boat to see the city's skyline and famous sights from the sea. Explore the Dolmabahçe Palace, an icon of Ottoman grandeur, and its rich interiors.

Afternoon: Visit Ortaköy, a vibrant area. Take a leisurely walk along the shoreline, see the Ortaköy Mosque, and savor some local street cuisine.

Evening: Enjoy Ortaköy's bustling nightlife, which includes exquisite cafés and bars overlooking the Bosphorus.

Day three: culinary delights and local

markets.

Morning: Explore Istanbul's culinary scene with a visit to the Grand Bazaar. Explore the maze-like passageways lined with spices, fabrics, and Turkish treats.

Afternoon: Visit the Spice Bazaar, a sensory feast including vendors selling spices, teas, and sweets. Enjoy a wonderful meal at one of the neighborhood restaurants.

Evening: Take a Turkish cooking lesson to master the techniques of producing traditional foods.

Day Four: Exploring Neighborhoods

Morning: Explore Kadıköy, a bustling Asian neighborhood. Explore the markets, fashionable cafés, and street art.

Afternoon: cross the Bosphorus to Beşiktaş. Visit the Dolmabahçe Clock Tower and take a leisurely walk along the shoreline.

Evening: Enjoy the vibrant atmosphere of Beşiktaş's restaurants and pubs.

Day Five: Arts and Culture

Morning: Visit the Istanbul Modern Art Museum to learn about current Turkish art.

Afternoon: Visit the historic quarter of Karaköy. Visit the Istanbul Museum of Modern Art and have a coffee at one of the stylish cafés.

Evening: Explore Karaköy's lively street art scene and have supper at a local restaurant.

Day Six: Relaxation and Wellness.

Morning: Escape to the Princes' Islands. Board a ferry to Büyükada, the biggest of the islands. Explore the lovely neighborhoods by horse-drawn carriage.

Afternoon: Spend a leisurely day by the shore, eating seafood at local eateries, and taking in the island's calm.

Evening: Return to the mainland and relax with a traditional Turkish bath experience.

Day Seven: Historic Districts, and Farewell

Morning: Visit the Chora Church, which is famous for its magnificent Byzantine mosaics.

Afternoon: Explore the old Balat area, which has colorful residences and bright street art.

Evening: Wrap out your trip to Istanbul with a goodbye meal at a rooftop restaurant, where you can enjoy panoramic city views.

Made in United States
Troutdale, OR
10/14/2024

23720240R00137